What Reader's are Say
Art of Dating and Attracting Women in Six Weeks

"*The Program* explores perhaps the most fascinating phenomenon of our time: Dating. And it does with an expert guide in Joseph Adago, who has plenty of secrets for building confidence and attracting women. This is a brilliant book."—*Kris, a 28 year old, Copywriter, from Williamsburg, Brooklyn.*

"As a woman, I found Joseph's book engaging and provocative. It's charming, smart, true-to-life and unexpectedly funny. The more guys who read this book the better!"—*Danielle, Artist, Greenpoint, Brooklyn.*

"*The Program* . . . provides invaluable step–by-step tools and perspective on dating that I'll use . . . . I've already suggested it to a couple of my single buddies."—*James, 33-year-old film maker from Parks Slope, Brooklyn.*

"An unbelievable book that every single guy should read, *The Program* lays out a system for dating that works."—*Nate, 34 year old contractor from Union City, New Jersey.*

"Joseph has hit the core of what it takes to be successful in the fast-paced dating world of today . . . . *The Program* is an excellent guide for men of all ages looking for more success in the dating world."—*Jeff, Advertising Salesman, Bedford-Stuyvesant, Brooklyn.*

"Reading *The Program* will show you the steps on gaining more confidence at finding the right woman for you. Even for those who think they know what a woman really wants in a man will gain some knowledge from reading this book. Every single guy should have this book!"—*Steve, 34, Kensington (Brooklyn), Freelance Writer.*

". . . an excellent guide—practical, level-headed, insightful . . . the book is full of useful, realistic suggestions. I wish I had read this book twenty years ago—I think I'd be a happier man today."—*James, 39, college administrator, Hudson Valley New York.*

Also by Joseph Adago

How to Move to New York City, Forthcoming

THE PROGRAM

Joseph Adago

ISBN: 978-1-937327-095

Library of Congress Control Number: 2012943794
Also available in Kindle, Nook and ePub formats
Manufactured in the United States of America

Book design by Moonshine Cove; cover image Bigstock #30188435

For my mother and father, Cathy and John

Contents

Section One: The Principles and Practices of The Program

Section Two: Getting Dates and Dating

Section Three: How The Program Works Day to Day and a Schedule

Concluding Chapters

ACKNOWLEDGEMENTS

This book would not be possible without the following people, and I would like to thank them by name: To my old friend and fellow writer John who helped me immeasurably with his kind advice regarding writing and publishing. To Wendy for her patient editing and advice. To Chris my agent for working tirelessly to get this book published. To my good friends Alex, James, Josh and Marc who partially inspired this book. And finally to my new bride Olivia whose willingness to marry me made *The Program* a raving success before it was ever read by a single reader.

Section 1: The Principles and Practices of *The Program*

Chapter One
The Program

Hey, are you one of those guys who had a girlfriend ever since early high school? Maybe you dated the prom queen or a cheerleader? After that you always dated someone or for that matter a couple of someones without a break. Has your major problem with women been that they keep falling in love with you and trying to tie you down? Do you consider a dry spell to be a couple of days or maybe a long weekend? If this is you then I am going to save you a little time and a little money. Do not buy this book. Whatever you are doing is working just fine.

You see that guy who just put down this book and is now browsing a GQ magazine? He is very good at dating women. In this book we're going to study and dissect him and then beat him at his own game. This book is going to get you as good as him at dating and, for that matter, even better. Over the next six weeks I am going to guide and teach you how to be good at dating and attracting women...Really Good. In a nutshell, that is what *The Program* is all about.

This is how dating works by the numbers. Approximately fifteen percent of the single male straight population is really good at attracting women. The whole process just comes very naturally to them. When you hear beautiful women complaining about having no one to date they are not referring to typical guys, rather, they are referring to the guys in the fifteen percent group. In this book I am going to refer to this guy as Mr. Wonderful. The average pretty girl could scream out the window and land a date with a typical guy who would worship the ground she walks on. This girl, however, is inevitably not all that interested in the typical guy. She is trying to land a Mr. Wonderful. Mr. Wonderful is usually giving her a limited amount of a time because at any given moment he has a number of women vying for his attention.

Mr. Wonderful has been immortalized in books and movies such as *The Rules* and *He's Just Not That Into You*. Matt Leblanc plays him almost perfectly as Joey in *Friends* and there is no better depiction of him than Mr. Big in *Sex and The City*.

There are two other categories of single guys. One is a guy who attracts a girl early in his life, usually in high school or college. They date for a while; they might even break up and get back together but they eventually get married. This guy does spend a certain amount of time technically being single but he never really is. All I really have to say in this book to this guy is "Good luck and God Bless." The third category is comprised of guys who struggle with dating and attracting women to one degree or another. In this book I am calling him The Typical Guy.

The way this book came about is that I was returning from a short vacation and feeling kind of down. I realized that what I was feeling sad about was not my job, my friends or my family. Instead, it was my dating life. I took out a pad and began to list everything I had been told about dating and attracting women.

You just need more confidence, Joe.

That was true, but how do you maintain and promote that confidence?

You have a great personality, Joe. You should be just fine.

I did have a great personality, but I was not just fine. What I came to realize was that my personality with regards to women needed some important changes.

You need to get in better shape, Joe.

This was also true, but you know what? This actually was not one of the major items that was holding me back. What I found was most of what I had been told was somewhat true but very incomplete.

I then began writing notes on everything I had witnessed about dating and attracting women. I always had a lot of male friends. Some of them were really good with women and Mr. Wonderful is a composite of them. I studied their actions. This yielded a lot of answers. I then laid out a practical plan for change.

The result is *The Program*, a step-by-step, day-by-day guide which will revolutionize your dating life. *The Program* is something like a diet or a workout regime, except instead of better abs or losing a couple pounds it is going to, in the coming weeks, transform you into a guy who excels at dating and attracting women. The bad news about *The Program* is it does not consist of one rule which you repeat over and over. If this were a diet book this would not be the diet book that just tells you over and over not to eat carbohydrates. In other words, you cannot just read one chapter, skim a couple more and get the general idea. You have to read the whole book.

The good news about *The Program* is that you have everything you need to succeed at dating. You do not have to look like Brad Pitt or be as rich as Donald Trump. When I developed and I applied *The Program*, I was somewhat overweight and actually in the worst financial shape I had been in years and I was flabbergasted at how well I did with women. Another good thing about *The Program* is it does not consist of you approaching girls at bars and clubs. In fact, at the beginning I would completely discourage you from doing this. This book clocks in at an easy to read one hundred and sixty seven pages. It has three sections, plus several concluding chapters. The first part lays out the principles and practices of *The Program*. The second part shows you how to meet and date a lot of women so you can practice and master *The Program* and the third portion consists of a practical, step-by-step schedule for starting and succeeding with *The Program*.

Are you excited? You should be. This is going to be a blast—let's get started.

Chapter Two

The Typical Guy's First Mistake

Single women are just as confounded and desperate to find someone as you are. The way the dating world works now is not doing them any favors either. They are just confounded in different ways.

When I was writing this book I went to the relationships section in a major book store near where I live to buy a copy of *The Rules*. I bought it because I wanted to see the other side of the equation. Before I went to pay for the book at the register, I found a seat facing the section and took out a pad and began to work on this book. In two hours I saw a fair amount of men looking at relationship books but I saw even more women. Most women are attracted to a small percentage of men and they want a monogamous relationship. Obviously if ninety-five percent of the single women are chasing fifteen percent of the men this is going to be a fairly frustrating process for most women. Most single women are upset because they are struggling to land or hold on to a Mr. Wonderful. If that fails, they are trying to convince themselves to settle for A Typical Guy who they are not all that attracted to.

What had to be the most painful conversation of my life occurred with a girl who I was in love with and was desperately trying to have as my girlfriend. When I literally begged her to see me in a different light she said, "I tried

Joe, I tried." And you know she had tried. We must have gone out fifty times. I could not have worked any harder at chasing her. Every time she called I dropped whatever I was doing and ran to her. I wracked my brains trying to find a way to get her to like me the way I wanted her to like me. But I acted like A Typical Guy around her and in the end she liked me and at some level she may have even loved me but she was not attracted to me.

Almost every Typical Guy has experienced the following situation: You take a girl out, she talks with you, laughs with you, drinks with you and she seems to be having a great time and then you call her the next day to ask her out again and she turns you down. You ask yourself "What went wrong?" She seemed to have a good time. She seemed to really like you. She seemed to think you were a great guy. The answer is she did have a good time, she did really like you and think you were a great guy but she was not attracted to you. And you made some mistakes.

What *The Program* is teaching you is to attract girls. Having a girl really like you and think you are a great guy is not the same as being attracted to you. The Typical Guy works hard to get a woman to like him. He should be working to get her to be *attracted* to him. I once knew a piano player who used bad techniques and did not take instruction at all. He spent a lot of time banging away at the piano. He worked hard and he never became a very good pianist. Before *The Program* I related somewhat to the poor guy. Which leaves me to ask the following question: Who Is Mr. Wonderful and Why Does He Attract Women?

Chapter Three

Who Is Mr. Wonderful And Why Does He Attract Women?

There is a television show on *Bravo* called *Millionaire Match maker* and it is fascinating. It usually takes two rich, relatively good looking men and sets them up on dates with pretty women. Even though these guys are presented in the best possible light they often fail to impress their dates. These guys on paper should be Mr. Wonderfuls. But they are not.

Until I started *The Program* I always assumed that the guys who were really good with women were either really good looking or really rich. I was pretty shocked to find that this was definitely not the case. Of the twenty guys I knew, I classified four of them as Mr. Wonderfuls. None of these guys were extraordinarily good looking. None of them spent hours upon hours in the gym. The best looking, most in shape guys I knew struggled with dating. Nor were the Mr. Wonderfuls I knew rich. About four years ago at the height of the real estate boom I was probably the richest guy amongst my circle of friends. I drove a luxury car and I lived in a luxury apartment with a river view in Manhattan. I sure as hell was not a Mr. Wonderful. In fact, I was the worst amongst my friends at dating and attracting women.

So if Mr. Wonderful is neither the best looking guy we know nor the richest then why is he landing so many girls?

Here is a list of the eight qualities that make Mr. Wonderful so attractive to women.

1) He is confident when dealing with women and that confidence shows. In *The Program* you are going to learn to develop this sort of confidence and you are going to learn to project this confidence.

2) He is funny and charming when around women. You are going emulate that. In this book we are going to work to improve your dating personality.

3) He dates a lot of women. This makes sense. He is good at dating women because he dates a lot of women. How do you get good at something? You do it over and over. In *The Program* you go on two to three dates a week. I know what you are thinking: "How the hell am I going to get two to three dates a week?" Don't worry, it's not that hard. I will show you how. There is a second aspect to this and it is one of the more important things to note.

4) Women are attracted to Mr. Wonderful because they think a lot of other women are attracted to him. In other words, women like men who date a lot of women. I have devoted a full chapter in this book to this quality. In *The Program* I will refer to the fourth quality as The Quality.

5) He dresses sharply, keeps himself well groomed and has found a look that works for him. Without any drastic changes we are going to take your appearance up several notches.

6) He handles rejection well. It is not that Mr. Wonderful does not get rejected, it's just that he lets it roll off his back. Getting rejected sucks. It is the reason so many people hate dating. I am going to show you how to minimize the pain of rejection and quickly move on.

7) When he meets a girl he likes he chases her in a disciplined fashion. When he gets her email address he emails her quickly. When he gets her number he calls her quickly. He returns emails and phone calls in a timely fashion. I know what I am saying somewhat defies conventional wisdom. In this case the conventional wisdom is wrong and I am right.

8) Mr. Wonderful may make it look easy but he works hard at dating and attracting women. Dating and attracting women takes some time, some work, and some discipline. You have to make dating and attracting women a priority.

I have dedicated full chapters to some of these qualities. All of these qualities are emphasized throughout the book. In *The Program* you are going to practice and master these qualities. There is a ninth quality.

9) Mr. Wonderful thrives at bars and clubs.

And you know what? He can have them. This is one area where at least in the beginning we are not going to emulate Mr. Wonderful.

When you watch the guys on *Millionaire Matchmaker* you can pick up a lot about what they are doing wrong. I am actually far more interested in what they are doing right. The major thing they are doing right is that they are not looking to pick up girls at bars or clubs. Instead, they are improving their odds by going another route. I know what you are thinking, "I do not have ten thousand dollars laying around to join *Millionaire Matchmaker*. That's cool, neither do I. In this book I am going to teach you to get dates on internet dating sites, singles events, parties and other events where you can succeed more easily at attracting women.

You might have already tried some singles events and had less than stellar results. With *The Program* you are going to pick up skills that will lead to stellar results. You might also be thinking that you have tried *Match.com* or another internet dating site and you did not do that great there either. Don't worry about it. I'm not going to just teach you to be good at internet dating; I'm going to teach you to master it.

Chapter Four

The Quality

If you took a group of single men and gave them truth serum and asked them what quality they initially found most attractive in a woman the answer would always be the same: Her looks. If you did the same with women you would get a variety of answers. Here is my answer: The quality that women initially find most attractive in a man is their ability to attract a lot of women. I will refer to this as The Quality.

In high school it is very obvious to the girls which boys attract a lot of girls. A teenage girl's dating pool basically consists of her high school and it is very easy for her to detect which boys have The Quality. A teenage boy who splits with his pretty cheerleader girlfriend always has her equally pretty friends throwing themselves at him shortly afterward. This is basically the plot of the 80s teen classic *Can't Buy Me Love*. Ronald is a smart geek with no social life who pays the prettiest girl in school to pretend to go out with him for a month. He tells her that just by dating him she will make him popular. He is right and when they "break up" he immediately starts dating her popular friends.

I would wager that most women would never admit to themselves that The Quality is important to them. I remember one time I was hanging out drinking late into the night with two very pretty girls. The girl I was interested in, who was at this point really drunk, said to her friend, "I want to end up with a man who has been with a lot of women." (Actually she used a far cruder term). I do not think she would have said this if she were sober.

This of course creates a catch-22 situation for The Typical Guy who is starting *The Program*. If you do not possess The Quality how are you supposed to attract women? It is very important that women PERCEIVE that you have The Quality. In other words, in the beginning of *The Program* you are going to have to fake it. To quote William Shakespeare, "assume a virtue if you have none."

Part of convincing women that you possess The Quality has nothing to do with your actual dating history. By acting with confidence, by speaking well and by dressing well you are actually sending out signals that you have The Quality. Most couples who first start dating tend to dance around the subject of past relationships. Generally the topic comes up briefly on the first date and a bit more on the second date.

This leads us to you discussing your dating history. If the two of you are not dating exclusively, discussing other women you are currently dating is pretty much an off limits discussion. Women also do not want to hear all the gory details of your previous relationship. When you start *The Program,* if you have never had a real long-term girlfriend, don't worry about it. Just never indicate this to any girl you are interested in. Women like men who are good at dating other women. Which means telling her what a failure you were with women in the past is absolutely forbidden. I would not mention this book either. You want her to think you are a Mr. Wonderful. And you know what? By the time you are done with *The Program* you will be. When discussing your last relationship you should say that you broke up with her and that it occurred within the last year. When you admit that you got dumped or that you do not have much experience with relationships you are indicating that you do not have The Quality. Never ever indicate that you have trouble attracting women.

This is really the only place in the book where I may be suggesting a small fib. I will point out that women generally also fib in this area as well, but in a different way. It is a rare woman that will admit to sleeping with numerous men. *Cosmopolitan* once published an article in which they suggested that women should admit to having only slept with three men to their partner. Telling the truth did not seem to be the article's biggest priority.

My sister once told me a story about meeting a guy at a party. He was a bit out of shape, was sort of a slacker work-wise and was slightly younger then my sister preferred, but she said she could tell by the way he held himself and spoke that he was really good with women. She ended up chasing him a little, getting his number, setting up a date with him and then he backed away from her. My sister is beautiful, charming and very together. This guy was sort of a mess but she was chasing him. He had The Quality. A large portion of this book is written to show you how to convey to women that you have The Quality.

Meanwhile, in *The Program*, from the way you talk, to the way you dress, to the way you present your past relationships, you are working hard to convey that you possess The Quality. For a variety of reasons she is not going to grill you on whether you went to prom with the head cheerleader. If a girl goes out with Mr. Wonderful she realizes during the course of dinner that he has The Quality and is most likely attracted to him. If a girl goes out with

The Typical Guy she realizes over the course of dinner that he does not have The Quality and is most likely not attracted to him. Once you have engaged in *The Program* for a couple of months you are a Mr. Wonderful. In the beginning of *The Program* you are in a gray area and in a sense you are jamming your date's radar.

In a bar or club setting it is very easy for women to pick up which men possess The Quality. In other words, in these settings women can fairly easily detect which men are able to attract other women and which men are not. And this is one of the reasons I am rather indifferent towards the idea of you trying to pick up girls in these settings when you are first learning *The Program*. Once you have mastered *The Program* you will do just fine at bars and clubs.

Chapter Five

What The Typical Guy is doing to Make Himself Unattractive to Women

Before feminism, a guy and girl dated generally with the same goal in mind. They were going to get married and raise kids. He was going to be the breadwinner; her primary responsibility would be the house and the children. Whether this was a good or bad thing is a debate for another book. The Typical Guy with regards to dating has purposely misread feminism.

If you interviewed a twenty-five year old single woman from 1950 and then another twenty-five year old single woman from 2010 you would find that what they are looking for in a mate is remarkably similar. Both want to have kids. Both would value family. Both would expect that in the future their husband is going to be the primary bread winner and both would expect that the kids and the family would be their primary responsibility. The qualities that a woman would look for in a mate in the 50s and now *have not changed nearly as much as The Typical Guy thinks.*

Women want to be with a man who can protect and care for them. If a woman wants to date another woman she will. A woman wants to date a guy who acts like a man, not a wimp. Women are attracted to men who display leadership. Why do you think most women end up marrying men who are a bit older than them? Why do rich older CEOs hook up with pretty twenty-five years old? Why, despite rather draconian sexual harassment laws, is it still pretty common for female underlings to sleep with their bosses? Not long ago it came out that David Letterman carried on numerous affairs with much younger women who worked under him, apparently both literally and figuratively.

I once heard a professor at a prestigious university on the radio promoting her book in which she argued that women should marry men that were significantly beneath them career wise. While listening to the interview I was thinking that she must have married a waiter or a pizza delivery guy. And I was surprised to discover at the end of the interview that she had chosen as a husband a man who was a professor at the same prestigious university where she worked. If I recall correctly he was even a bit older then her. Here is a woman who had written an entire book arguing that women should choose a husband who they would not look up to yet she herself could not bring herself to marry a man who was socially or financially beneath her.

The Typical Guy knows that women are attracted to men that display leadership. He also knows that women are looking for a guy who acts like a man and gives off the vibe that he can protect and care for her. The Typical Guy fears the type of single woman who he is attracted too. He is afraid to ask her out, he is afraid of offending her and he is afraid that she will dump him. The result of this fear is *fear based behavior*. The Typical Guy displays fear based behavior in some of the following ways:

He puts himself down. He usually makes jokes at his own expense and tells stories that make him look bad.

He lives in mortal fear of somehow offending her and he acts like it.

He puts her on a pedestal.

He is polite to her to the point of ridiculousness. "Thank you so much for calling me back."

He kisses up to her.

He showers her with compliments.

He bends over backward to accommodate her.

He tells her how lucky he is to be dating a girl like her. This also violates the rules laid out regarding The Quality.

He tells her how much he loves her way before it is appropriate.

He acts nervous when he first approaches her, thus almost guaranteeing that he will be shot down.

He tries to buy her affection. By getting her fancy gifts or taking her out to really pricey places.

All of the above self-defeating behaviors have to stop. *At every step of dating*, fear based behavior must be avoided. How is a woman supposed to look up to a man if she senses that he is afraid of her? How is she supposed to think that this man will be able to care for her and her future children if he is afraid of her? If women sense this fear, it is the kiss of death for a guy who is interested in her.

To summarize this chapter: Women are attracted to men who display leadership and therefore, so should you. However, make sure you do not misunderstand this chapter and get the impression that you should be acting like a sexist pig. First, this is just wrong. And second, it is obviously very unattractive. You should always act like a gentleman. I also do not want you to get the impression that in order to display leadership you have to be the president of Exxon. Later in this book I will write about how you should speak about your job with regards to leadership and also some ideas for displaying leadership.

Chapter Six

Improving Your Dating Personality

People often told me I had a good personality and, in a way, they were right. I was funny, kind and certainly well read. I always had a lot of friends, and for a guy who seldom dated, I had a remarkably busy social calendar. When I started to examine my personality I discovered that I had two personalities, a friend personality and a dating personality. My friend personality was pretty good. My dating personality needed some changes. Your dating personality is how you act, speak, communicate and carry yourself in front of women who you are dating or are interested in dating. In this chapter I am going to show you how to improve your dating personality.

   I am going to start this chapter by discussing humor, which is a key weapon with regards to attracting women and, for many Typical Guys, is also their Achilles Heel. Humor is important but many guys will go with a self-depreciating type of humor. They will tell stories and jokes in which they put themselves down. This is entertaining but very unattractive. Do not do this...ever. This is one of the major mistakes that Typical Guys make with women.

   It is important to be funny and entertaining and just as important to not put yourself down. You will be surprised how easy it is to change your sense of humor. A lot of Typical Guys are actually pretty funny. Like most Typical

Guys who are funny, I had a very self-depreciating sense of humor; however, when I realized that this was doing me way more harm than good I stopped telling funny stories which made me look bad. I was actually surprised how easy it was to remain funny and entertaining without criticizing myself.

Tease your date a little. This is very effective because girls are so used to being kissed up to that it actually makes you stand out a bit. There is a fine line between making fun of your date in a light-hearted way and in a cruel way. Make sure you are doing the former. If you tease a girl with an incredible body when she mentions dieting, that's fine. Teasing a girl who is struggling with her weight, well, I am sure you realize that's not fine, at all.

Your sense of humor is something that should be worked on and improved in general. If you have friends who are funny, watch how they tell stories and jokes and then replicate the process. If you have a friend who is a Mr. Wonderful, hang out with him in social settings and take note as to how he uses humor when he is with women. You should also TiVo some standup comedy routines on cable, study them and maybe even borrow a bit of their material.

The rest of this chapter consists of some general rules: Do not put yourself down. I know I already mentioned this with regards to humor but it's a point well worth mentioning again for emphasis. This was a major fault of mine. I would tell entertaining stories but I would often include a story in which I looked bad. When I started to improve my dating personality I stopped this self-defeating behavior. You must do the same.

Hold yourself with a sense of confidence that borders on swagger. Whether you are on a date with a woman or approaching a woman, hold yourself with extreme confidence. The attitude you are trying to convey is that you are good at what you are doing and you enjoy what you are doing. Be upbeat, not gloomy. Your date does not want to hear what an awful jerk your roommate is or how much you hate your boss. Nor does she want to hear how your ex-girlfriend broke your heart in a million pieces. And you already know she doesn't want to hear what a loser you are with women.

Be entertaining. Tell a funny story about your jerky roommate but do not follow it up with a diatribe about how much you hate him. You can also tell a funny story about your boss but you want to give the overall impression that you enjoy your work.

Don't come off as an angry guy. Do not go off on diatribes about women, your mother, politics, religion or anything else. Don't let yourself sound whiny. Do not whine about women, your mother or anything else.

Don't be annoying. When men feel the need to speak just to fill in time they tend to say stupid things. Look, a little silence is not that terrible. Far worse is annoying her. If you are on a date and a girl does not want to talk about the job that she is leaving, drop the subject. If you tell a joke that goes the wrong way do not repeat it. This sounds obvious but it is something to be aware of and avoid. I bet you do this more than you think.

You should be developing a Dating Act. When you are on a date you see what works and when you get a good reaction use the same story with a future date. Mr. Wonderful understands this. When I was out with him at bars meeting women he told great stories and they were well rehearsed. And you know what? They were a joy to listen to. At one point I was discussing with Mr. Wonderful a surprise wedding in Barcelona that a friend had thrown for his wife which we all attended. "Oh," he said "that is a first date story." On the next date I went on I worked that story into the conversation and it got a great reaction. That story became part of my Dating Act.

Always give your date your full attention. I once dated a girl who used to poke me when I was not listening to what she was saying, which I found kind of endearing, but it also made me realize that I needed to listen more fully. I always noticed that when Mr. Wonderful spoke to a woman, he concentrated on nothing but her. Women find this quality irresistible. When you are out with a girl try to minimize the drinking. You want to stay awake and in control. I know this can be tricky as dating these days tends to go hand in hand with a fair amount of alcohol.

Work on becoming a more interesting and dynamic person. Once on a date a girl asked me what I did for fun. I stuttered for a second and then said something about watching TV and reading. I did not hit the ball out of the park with that is answer. When I started *The Program* I thought about that incident and made an effort to do some activities that would make me a more interesting, well rounded person and a better date. I began doing volunteer tutoring at an after school program. I also joined a book club. I enjoyed both activities and they also made me a more interesting date. You should look into joining activities that you enjoy: take a cooking class, join a book club, do volunteer work, go skydiving, whatever appeals to you.

My best friend is a computer guy. Like many computer guys he was not all that into reading. He was always charming and well spoken but I very clearly remember when he graduated from college he subscribed to *Newsweek* and spent thirty minutes every week reading it. He saw a weakness in his personality and consciously made an effort to fix it. And it worked. To this day he comes off as very well read.

Let's go over a couple of subjects to steer clear of on a date. Like about eighty percent of men on this planet, I am a little obsessed with professional sports. But I would keep the sports talk to minimum. Most women get really bored when hearing a ten minute diatribe on why the New York Mets should fire their GM. Other subjects that are best left alone are science fiction movies, TV and video games. Again, these are subjects that tend to appeal to men and tend to bore women to tears. I actually think that video games and science fiction are subjects that should not be brought up at all as they tend to indicate to women that you are a loser.

Go on a lot of dates. How do you improve your dating personality? You date a lot. The reason Mr. Wonderful does so well at dating is that he practices a lot. This makes sense. The way you get good at anything is you practice it over and over.

When I first started *The Program* I went on a date with a girl who was very nice but was not my type. I knew she would go out with me, but I did not call to ask her out again. This was a mistake for two reasons. The first is that in *The Program*, especially in the beginning, one of the reasons you are dating is to improve your dating personality. The best way to do this is go out on a lot of dates. The second reason is that men in general and definitely Typical Guys put way too much stock into first impressions. In this regard men are actually much worse than women. Oddly, The Typical Guy tends to be far choosier than Mr. Wonderful. This is kind of strange. It is sort of like a starving guy insisting that he will only eat at three star French restaurants. Mr. Wonderful once commented to me, "You know for a guy who doesn't date a lot you sure have high standards."

Who knows? Maybe the girl that you reluctantly ask out on a second date turns out to be amazing and is the future Mrs. Not-So Typical.

Until your relationship with a girl is exclusive, keep on dating other people. The Typical Guy meets a girl he likes and then closes up the dating shop. Mr. Wonderful continues to date other women. Guess who is right? You may really like the girl but there is no guarantee that she is all that into you or she may have an on again, off again boyfriend who is suddenly back on again. By dating other women you are making yourself in demand. This makes you more confident and that confidence helps you improve your dating personality. Remember, women are attracted to men who attract other women. It also helps you avoid Fear Based Behavior.

Chapter Seven

Leadership and The Quality with Regards to The Dating Personality

A lot of improving your dating personality has to do with establishing leadership in a relationship and avoiding Fear Based Behavior. Establishing leadership when dating is a little tricky for the following reason: in dating and in every stage of courtship, women hold the balance of power which is probably why many sexist societies have established systems of arranged marriage, thus eliminating the whole courtship process. In a modern society it is ultimately the women who makes the decision on whether she will be with or remain with any particular man. A man asks a woman if she wants to give him her number. The man then calls and asks her out, a man will make the initial romantic pass at a women and a man proposes marriage to a women. At every stage of courtship the woman makes the final decision. Yet paradoxically, women are attracted to leadership. You are, therefore, not actually establishing leadership but rather the illusion of leadership.

A large part of establishing the appearance of leadership is done by displaying leadership. The man plans the date, the man pays for the date and, romantically, he makes the first move. This is what you should do. Before *The Program,* I used to ask a date whether she would prefer to go out to a French restaurant or an Italian place. This is wrong. Establish leadership by being decisive, pick a place that is nice and then take her there. When you approach a girl you should always ask for her number. Obviously you should not give her your number or your card. Getting her number puts you in control which is attractive to women.

Always show up to a date ten minutes early. Women are often late. That is fine. But you are trying to establish yourself as the man in the relationship. This also gives you an opportunity to make sure the place you have chosen will work. I once was meeting a girl for a first date at a wine bar. When I got there the place was mobbed and there was a wait to get in. I quickly found a place nearby that was perfect for a first date and was not too crowded. When she called me to tell me she was running late I told her that the first place was too crowded but I had found a really cool place nearby. She complimented me for being so take-charge.

Remember that your mother taught you be a chivalrous, well-mannered, gentlemen. Hold the door open for your date and stand up when she walks into the room. This is very important because it allows you to emphasize gender roles. I tended to date women who were the hippy, yoga practicing type and therefore somewhat feminist leaning, but even they appreciated these qualities. Remember your manners. Hold your fork correctly, put your napkin on your lap before you eat and do not talk with your mouth full. When you speak do not to use profanity or crude language. Always walk a girl to her door, to her car or help her hail a cab.

When you discuss your career, spin it in a positive light. Remember women want to be able to admire men with whom they are with. This does not mean you have to be a CEO of a Fortune 500 company—most men are not. If you are a schoolteacher, talk about how much you enjoy your job and how you really feel that you make a difference. Also tell her you are taking classes towards a masters degree and intend to eventually become a principal. Women want to see that you are working toward a future.

When Mr. Wonderful was first dating the woman who he would eventually marry he was also just starting up his own business. He told me his then girlfriend Jenny bought the dream. When I talked with him about his work he usually complained how difficult it was. However, when he talked with women he spoke about how excited he was about the future. In fact this version of his career was true, and today his business is very successful. He also has a wonderful wife.

Avoid Fear Based Behavior at all costs. Do not put women on a pedestal. Do not go on and on about how wonderful they are. In fact, in the beginning do not give women compliments. Do not fall in love. Do not think about her. Do not tell yourself or anybody else that a particular girl is out of your league. Before *The Program,* I told Mr. Wonderful about a girl I really liked. "Why do you like her?" he asked. I told him that for starters, I thought she was totally out of my league. "Joe," he said "What the hell does that even mean?" Exactly! Such talk is nothing but Fear Based Behavior, which must be avoided.

In Chapter Four we discussed how to talk about past relationships but there are a couple of other items with regards to your dating personality and this subject. Women are both hesitant and compelled to talk with men about their past relationships. They are hesitant because other women have warned them to avoid the subject. They are compelled because past relationships very much define for them the life they have led. The first mistake men make in this situation is to act uncomfortable and change the subject. If a girl brings up the subject, talk to her a bit about it, ask some questions, let her express her emotions and show some sympathy. Don't be afraid of her emotions. The second mistake men make in this situation is to become emotional themselves and bring up a past relationship in which they got their heart broken. DO NOT DO THIS! Talking about your emotions is bad! You often hear women who are in long-term relationships complain that their partner will not open up emotionally. Actually one of the reasons that smart men do not open up emotionally, even to long-term girlfriends, is that they have learned the hard way and know they get dumped when they do. Opening up like this is a giant mistake because when you let them know your heart was broken you are telegraphing to them that you do not have The Quality.

The final point on this subject is that you do not want to oversell it. Jabbering on and on about other women, real or otherwise, is a bad idea. When a girl in a conversation brings up a past relationship you should at some time in the conversation mention a past girlfriend—just don't get all teary eyed about it, and don't let on that she dumped you.

Chapter Eight

Look Sharp: Improve The Way You Look

I once saw an interview in which a minor celebrity was asked why he had such a reputation as a lady's man. He replied that it was not that he was that great but he dressed well and was well groomed and that when he went out the guys around him helped by looking like slobs. Obviously he was exaggerating but he had a good point. In this chapter, we are going to get you looking more like the lady's man and less like the slobs around him.

We will start with your clothes. Put together two or three outfits that are reserved for when you go out on dates or to singles events. Go through your closet and pick out the three best shirts and the three best pairs of pants. Wash and iron them, make sure they fit well and then line them up together. These are your date clothes and you should wear them when you go on dates or when you are out and there is a potential to meet women. Do not wear these clothes casually or at work. You want to keep these clothes in top condition.

When it comes to dressing you want to be neat, ironed and together. Always wear a belt. Make sure your belt and your shoes are the same color and make sure that color is black. Do not wear shorts on dates unless that date is to the beach. If you want to wear jeans, that is fine as long as you look good in them. Your jeans should be in good shape.

Save the torn pair of jeans for football in the park. Shirts that are intended to be tucked in should be tucked in. If you think that this over-emphasizes your waist, wear a blazer, or go with a polo style shirt that is meant to be un-tucked.

If you are going to buy some new clothes keep the following in mind. Buy pants that fit comfortably. When you buy pants you generally have to get them tailored to meet your exact length. Pants sometimes get scraggly at the bottom. If this happens you should get them hemmed. Buy clothes with outfits in mind. I usually went with dark colored polo shirts and matched them up either with khaki, tan, or dark colored slacks.

As far as designer brands go I would buy them with care. If you buy a shirt with a Polo logo or alligator logo on it, that is good, it shows status. However, the most important thing is that the shirt looks good on you. The logo is just gravy. Do not waste money on designer socks, boxers, pants or any other piece of clothing where women cannot tell they are designer. When you buy these items just make sure that they look good on you. The one exception to this rule is jeans. Designer jeans are not a waste of money. But again, the most important thing is that the jeans look good on you.

You should reserve one pair of shoes for when you go out socially. They should be black. You do not have to spend a ton of money on your shoes. They just have to be nice looking and well maintained. I have a nice pair of slip-on Steve Madden shoes, which I bought at Filene's basement for around seventy dollars and they were perfect for dating. I had them shined every three weeks and I would brush them up a little before I went out. Always match your black shoes with black socks and a black belt. You should purchase a shine sponge.

I can't believe I have to write this but I just read a blog by a girl who complained about guys on dates who made the following mistake. When you wear shoes obviously wear them with dress socks. Do not wear them with white socks. Also, wear shoes, not sneakers.

Wear a watch with a silver or gold band that looks nice. It does not have to cost you a lot of money. Absolutely no sport watches with rubber bands. The dial of the watch should be black, blue, gold or white, not red, orange, green or brown. I have two watches, both which cost me about four hundred dollars. One is a conservative Movado, which has a black dial and a silver band. The other is a divers watch I saw advertised in GQ Magazine and decided it looked cool. The divers watch has a rubber band and a bright orange dial. When I started *The Program* I stopped wearing the divers watch and just wore the Movado. If I ever decide to take up diving I will be sure to bring the divers watch along. If money is an issue I would recommend you spend about one hundred dollars on a watch. If you go to EBay you can find nice looking, appropriate watches in this price range on any given day.

If you do decide to spend in the three to six hundred dollar-range for your watch first and foremost make sure the watch is sharp and professional looking. In this price range make sure that you get a watch brand that women have heard of. A good rule of thumb before buying a watch in this price range is to page though *Newsweek*, *GQ* and *Esquire*. If you do not see the watch advertised in one of these magazines, do not buy it. If you have never heard of a particular watch brand, the odds are, neither has she.

If you are going to spend over four thousand on a watch I have one word for you, "Rolex." A Rolex is the Coco-Cola of luxury watches and she will notice it. Again get a conservative, sharp looking Rolex with the right color dial and silver, gold or a gold/silver band. For around three thousand dollars you should be able to buy a good looking pre-owned Rolex. For five thousand dollars and beyond you can get a new Rolex.

Your hair should be neat and slightly on the short side. Find a hair style that looks sharp. Your sideburns should be moderate in length and never choose a style that even hints of a mullet. You do not have to go to a fancy salon. Find someone local who does a good job. Then go to the local guy every three weeks. Guys tend to look sloppy when they wait too long to get a haircut. I used to spend seventy dollars to get my hair cut but I would only get my hair cut every six weeks or so. The result was I looked good for three weeks and then my hair looked too long and sloppy for three weeks. I found someone more affordable and I now get my hair cut every two weeks, and my hair looks neat all the time. If you are balding either go with the shaved look (women seem to love this look for men) or keep your hair very short. Buy some hair gel and a comb and use both of them. Before you go out apply gel and comb your hair. When you leave the house your hair should not be plastered to your head, but it should be neat.

If you wear glasses switch to contacts. Contacts look much better than glasses. If you are like me and you cannot wear contacts, wear stylish, rimless glasses. This is one place where you should spend a bit of money. The rimless glasses are the nicest and they are easy to keep clean. When you shop for glasses choose carefully. You should definitely seek out female advice.

Shave in the morning and shave before you go out socially. As of this writing, the five o' clock shadow look is slightly in. You might want to experiment with it but even then shave in the morning and then just do not shave before you go out. I occasionally went with this look, usually when my skin was a little less clear then I would have liked. Most of the time, however, I stuck to the clean shaven look. Buy a trimmer and use it. You should not have any hair in your nose or ears, check and then check them again. You should prune your eyebrows slightly, in other words, you should not have bushy eyebrows. Always clip your nails every other day and before you go out socially.

My skin was not terrible but it was not perfect either. When I started *The Program* I bought Stridex cleaning pads and applied them twice a day. This kept my skin fairly clear. If you suffer from acne that is worse than this go to the doctor and get the medicated pads, the pills or both. It is very, very important that you keep your skin clear.

Before you go out shower yourself to death. You should scrub your whole body with scented soap twice. You should then scrub your body thoroughly with body wash. Wash your hair twice. Use a deodorant with an antiperspirant and then apply cologne. Do not soak yourself with the cologne but do apply a moderate amount. Find cologne that is reasonably priced and appealing.

Keep your teeth in good shape. Brush them thoroughly three times a day. Go to the dentist and get them cleaned. The dentist usually recommends you get your teeth cleaned twice a year. I usually get my teeth cleaned three times a year. Experiment with some whitening kits. Ask your dentist to sell you one (they usually have the best). Buy some mouthwash and use it liberally before you go out. Always bring mints on dates or when you go out socially.

A friend of mine moved back home with her parents and her younger brother because of the economy. She said she had a ritual with her brother in which she would look him over before he went out on a date. She would almost inevitably send him back to his room to iron his pants or comb his hair. She was a really good sister. Before you go out you should stand in the mirror and replicate this process. I always would budget in an extra ten minutes before I went out in case I forgot something. Once you have looked yourself over, leave the house with a sense of confidence. Remember that at this point you are better dressed then ninety percent of the guys out there.

Some books on dating such as *The Game* or *The Mystery Method* recommend that you wear items that stand out. This is called the "Peacock Effect." The idea is to wear bright jewelry or a showy hat that makes you stand out. My advice regarding this is to give it a try and see if it works for you. It was not for me but it might work for you.

You have to work to find a style that is right for you. To do this might take a bit of research, a bit of experimenting and some work. I cannot say I have any love of fashion but I started buying the occasional issue of *Esquire* and *GQ* magazine with an eye toward improving the way I dressed.

If I saw a stylish guy on the subway I would study him for a minute and try to pick up why it was that I thought he was stylish. In general, I recommend that you dress up slightly. The look that worked for me was mostly nice polo type shirts and khaki or dark colored pants, but a different look might work better for you. If you go shopping for new clothes, you might take along a female friend or your sister as a fashion consultant.

The third section of this book looks at what we have discussed in this chapter from a scheduling perspective. Start by making some changes and then each week make an effort to add an item or two towards improving your appearance. With regards to clothing I started with my date clothes and then improved how I dressed overall. If you are self-employed or work for a company that has a dress casual policy you might start by buying an affordable suit or two and then wear them to work without a tie. You can iron the suit the night before and then have it dry cleaned once a week. The result is you always look sharp in case you meet someone you are interested in. When you buy a suit find a place that sells moderately priced suits where the salesmen actually advise you on what suit you should buy. With regards to your appearance it helps to be highly organized. I would devote one closet only to your date clothes. For your grooming items, put them all in one drawer. This way before a date you are not running around like a mad man trying to find your hair gel.

You might be reading this and thinking "I am doing a decent amount of this already." That will not fly. You must do as much of the above as possible and as soon as possible.

Chapter Nine

You Are Overweight, So You Get Your Own Chapter—Don't Worry You Can Still Succeed at The Program

You are overweight and you get depressed because you think your weight is keeping you from dating. The result is you self-medicate by eating too much which paradoxically causes you to be overweight. I have been there, my friend, and it sucks. You should not worry because we are going to get you out of this mess.

When I started *The Program* I was about fifty pounds heavier then I should have been and you know what? It was not a deal breaker. I was surprised at how many dates I went on. I was also surprised at how many second, third and fourth dates I went on. That said, being overweight definitely made dating tougher. One of the things that we talk about in *The Program* is building and maintaining confidence and if you are moving in the right direction with your weight this helps your confidence. I am sure you know this from past experience.

Start *The Program* and also go on a weight reduction program at the same time. Go out and join Weight Watchers, attend the weekly meetings and follow the rules like it is a religion...a really strict fundamentalist religion. Do not diet on your dates, just eat and drink moderately and then factor in your point intake. There are of course many other fine weight loss programs besides Weight

Watchers out there such as Jenny Craig and Nutrasystem®. If you find another weight loss program that works for you by all means go with it.

Don't start a weight reduction program with the intent of starting *The Program* in the future. Don't start *The Program* with the intent of starting a weight reduction program in the future. Start a weight reduction program and *The Program* at the same time. I can tell you from personal experience that it is much easier to follow a weight reduction program when you have three dates lined up in the next five days with three lovely women. A lot of overweight guys have had the experience of losing weight and then finding out much to their disappointment that they are still not having much luck with women. You need to improve both your dating skills with *The Program* and get in better shape.

When I started *The Program* I joined Weight Watchers. I also started a walking program in which I walked six miles a week. Later in *The Program* I started taking martial arts training, which I would also highly recommend. I would like to also mention a small positive note about this situation. I was amazed at how many pretty, single girls there were at any given Weight Watchers meeting. There had to be twenty girls for every guy at these meetings.

When you go to your weekly meeting, try to attend with a friend. I found this helped a lot because it added an element of peer pressure in a good way. There is nothing like a friendly rivalry to motivate you to improve.

If you struggle with your weight, dressing well becomes even more important. Do not wear clothes that are too tight. Dress conservatively and neatly, do not wear stripes and favor dark colored shirts. You do not have to be in perfect shape to succeed at *The Program.* You do need to be headed in the right direction.

Chapter Ten

How to Build and Maintain Confidence

Being confident and projecting confidence is vital when it comes to attracting women. There are several ways to build confidence. The first and easiest way is to succeed with women. Mr. Wonderful is confident when he approaches a woman because he has been successfully approaching women for as long as he has been interested in them. In the not too distant future as you work on and succeed in *The Program* you will also be able to draw on this sort of past success for confidence. Until then there are a number of other ways for you to gain confidence.

A very important part of *The Program* is that you take the glass half-full approach. Always strive to see the good in any situation. As I started to work my way through *The Program*, I was sitting at an almost empty bar. A couple of places away from me sat a girl who was reading Dan

Brown's latest book. I struck up a conversation with her about books, and before I left I asked for her number. She told me that she had a boyfriend. Instead of reflecting on the fact that she turned me down, I reflected on the fact that I had built my courage up enough to approach her, that I spoke to her with confidence and that I asked for her number. I had played my role well and done my job well. And I was sure that the next girl that I approached would give me her number, which, in fact, she did. This is the way you have to look at things in *The Program*, always the glass half full. When I would go out drinking with Mr. Wonderful and we were at a bar that was teeming with guys he would always say to me, "Come on, I bet the next bar is teeming with girls." This is the attitude you have to take when you are dating.

Try to reduce your caffeine, alcohol and sugar intake, eat more whole grains and vegetables and go easy on unhealthy foods in general. There is a book called *Fit for Life* by Harvey and Marilyn Diamond that is about eating in a more healthy fashion, and I highly recommend it. By leading a healthy balanced lifestyle you will have more energy and exhibit more confidence. Obviously, both these qualities, particularly the latter, are vital for achieving success in *The Program*.

If you are spiritual I also recommend attending weekly religious services in whatever tradition you are a part of. Part of living a balanced life should include the spiritual. It is worth noting that women tend to be more religious than men and therefore attend church in greater numbers than men, which means religious services and church activities are a pretty good place to meet women.

Confidence is like anything else, you improve it with practice. You do not exist in a vacuum. If you spend your time before a date seeing the worst in the world around you and acting without confidence in yourself, it is likely you will act the same way on your date. You should practice being confident and looking on the bright side. If you wake up with a sense of confidence, act with confidence at work and go home and get ready for your date with a sense of confidence the odds are very good that you will act with confidence that night on your date.

I would recommend that you start a martial arts program in order to build your confidence and to succeed in *The Program*. While you do not have to take up Martial Arts to succeed in *The Program* and in fact I did not start martial arts until I was doing *The Program* for a while, I think you will find it helpful even if you only do martial arts a couple times a week.

In order to stay in shape, you should be doing some sort of an exercise program anyway. Taking up martial arts is generally the same price of a monthly gym membership, so cost should not be that much of a burden. The type of martial arts program you choose makes no difference. Find the martial art that suits you best. Almost any martial arts school will give you a free introductory class. Most programs even offer some sort of affordable trial period. I tried out Judo and Taekwondo before discovering a Karate kick boxing school that was the perfect fit for me.

As I mentioned earlier, I started martial arts classes when I was several weeks into *The Program*. I was amazed at the difference it made in helping me build confidence, dating and attracting women. I suppose it's a weird example, but I felt like a baseball player who was hitting twenty homeruns a year who starts taking steroids and all of sudden starts hitting fifty homeruns a season, except I was actually making my body healthier rather than destroying it.

A martial arts program changes the way you look. You get muscular and lean which is obviously an incredible look for a guy looking to attract women. If you are doing *The Program* along with a weight loss program martial arts will help tremendously.

The benefits of a martial arts program with regards to *The Program* went way beyond the physical. I was surprised at what a perfect fit a martial arts program was with *The Program*. I am not sure there is a better way to build confidence then to train in the martial arts. When you start training in the martial arts it changes the way you hold yourself. Something about the way it affects your posture helps you exude confidence and swagger. Women want to be with a man who can protect them. There is no way better to send this vibe out then to take up the art of self-defense. Again, you are not required to do martial arts to succeed at *The Program* but I recommend it.

Chapter Eleven

Timing and Scheduling

A basic principle of *The Program* is proper time management. One of the mistakes men make with women is that in the beginning of the relationship they spend too much time with their dates. They make themselves appear to be clingy. The Typical Guy will often meet a girl at a party, spend the whole night hanging out with her and then call her the next day and get shot down. You want to limit the amount of time you spend with her thus preserving a sense of mystery.

Keep your dates with women on the short side. Instead of dinner and a movie just do dinner. If you meet a girl for a drink on a first date limit it to about an hour. When you speak to women on the phone, limit the amount of time. When you call a woman to ask her out on a date the phone call should not last more than twenty-five minutes. You actually want to end a date or conversation with her yearning for a bit more of your time. If you meet a girl at a bar talk for a bit and then make up an excuse to leave and then get her number. When you schedule dates at night generally schedule them for around 8:30 P.M., in other words, a bit on the late side. This allows you to end the date early without it appearing to be too early.

Years ago Mr. Wonderful gave me a bit of rather succinct advice. I had met a girl the night before and he asked if I had called her. I mumbled something about not wanting to appear too eager. He looked at me like I was crazy and said "What are you doing? Call her, call her quick." This bit of admonishment brings us to The 24 Hour Rule: If you meet a girl and get her number you have twenty-four hours to call her and ask her out. If you get her machine ask her to call you back, do not ask out her out on the machine. If she calls you and you miss her call, call her back as soon as possible. I cannot emphasize this point enough. How many times have you gotten a number from a girl, put off calling her for a day, then another day, then another and then you end up not calling her? I bet this has happened more then you want to think about. This is classic Typical Guy behavior and it has to stop. In *The Program*, The 24 Hour Rule is written in stone.

If, on an internet dating site you get an email from a girl, The 24 Hours Rule becomes The First Chance You Get Rule. This means you have two hours to respond to that email. In most cases I would make the case that you should answer the email as soon as you read it. If a girl gives you her email address The 24 Hour Rule converts to The 10 Hour Rule. You have ten hours to write her an email.

At the end of a date do not ask a girl if she wants to go out on another date. It makes you look needy, wait a day and then call her. You also want the girl to sweat it out a little about whether you will go out with her again. A good piece of general advice is not to get ahead of yourself. If you are emailing back and forth with a girl, do not ask her out in the email. Ask for her number and then call her, chat with her a little and then ask her out. The same goes for voicemail. If you call her and get her voicemail ask her to call you back but do not ask her out. Save asking her out for the actual conversation. After a first date The 24 Hour Rule converts to The 48 Hour Rule. That is you have forty-eight hours to call her and ask her out again.

Be vigilant about always answering your phone and not letting it go to voicemail. As much as possible, when a girl you are interested in calls you, you should pick up the phone and speak to her. By playing phone tag with a girl you are wasting time. When you get a girl's number immediately store her number in your phone so you will be able to recognize when she calls you and pick up.

When you approach a girl at a singles event or a bar, chat with her for no longer then fifteen minutes. Then either get her number or circle out and, as you are leaving, ask her for her number. In general when you are attending a singles event, I would subscribe to a strict 50 Minute Rule, that is attend the event for approximately 50 minutes, an hour at most. When you are out with your friends at a bar I would also subscribe to the 50 Minute Rule. When you are with friends going out to bars in order to meet women stay at any given bar for fifty minutes to an hour then hit the next bar. Obviously if there is the prospect of hooking up with someone the rule should go out the window.

Early in this book I mentioned that Mr. Wonderful has a reputation for not calling girls back and giving them a limited amount of attention. Do not do this at the beginning of a relationship. However, as the relationship progresses Mr. Wonderful in essence pulls back a bit. He starts calling her less. Ideally, he gets the relationship to the point where she is chasing him, which leads us to the concept of The 55 Hour Rule.

After you go out a couple times the 24 Hour Rule changes to the 55 Hour Rule. You want to leave her wondering a bit if you will call her. Ideally you want to get to a point where she starts calling you. One good indication that a girl you are dating is really into you is when she starts calling you more then you call her. If you are in a relationship for a month or so and you are still chasing her there is pretty good chance you are going to get dumped.

Regarding intimacy and timing, the standard advice in most dating books is not to move in too quickly. I am not sure if this is always correct. By the second date and sometimes even the first date, there should be some level of intimacy. Usually on the first date it's not a good idea to try to get too intimate. This, however, depends on the circumstance. I think a lot of Typical Guys tend to wait for a signal from the girl, violins to start playing or for the girl to make a pass at you. Most of the time, none of these things will happen. You just have to stick your neck out and kiss her.

Chapter Twelve

Big Moves: They Are not that Important

This book is primarily about things that you can change immediately. However, I am going to suggest changes that, if done correctly, will help you with dating. You are better off with roommates than living alone. It is also better to have roommates who are single. Women prefer men who are social. But the truth is I do not think it makes that much of a difference to women either way. And from a financial perspective you are far better off putting money into going out on lots of dates with women and dressing nicely then spending the extra money that it costs to live alone.

When it comes to choosing a place to live it should not be a wreck, but it also does not have to be amazing. The guy I know who was the best with women spent most of his single years living in a small two bedroom apartment where his Grandmother also lived. If a girl goes up to your apartment and starts fooling around with you, she is probably already pretty into you. To paraphrase Woody Allen "If you are a guy it does not matter if you are really good at sex because just by having it you have already won." If you do get a girl to your apartment make sure it is clean and that it smells nice.

I happen to live in one of the few places in America where you do not have to own a car. I have a pretty nice car, and I dated some girls in the suburbs. I am not sure how much difference it made. If you drive a really nice car it probably helps a little. Do not blab on and on about your car. Do not post up pictures of your car on your internet dating profile. You might tell a woman that you are really excited about your new car but then leave it at that. Women find car talk about as interesting as video games. That said do not drive a piece of junk. First of all, from a financial point of view, it makes no sense. I know from past experience that you end up spending so much money on repairs that you are better off driving a nicer car. Second, much like dressing sloppily, it gives a bad impression. The one exception to this is if you are a teenager or college student then having a car alone may be okay. Keep your car clean inside and out. The car I drove was a five year old top of the line Jeep Grand Cherokee that was in very good shape. It was not that expensive at all but looked sharp and worked fine for dating. Again I think you are better off spending your money on dates than on a new car. If money is not an issue then I would pick out a car that is sporty and really stands out: a sports car, a nice convertible or a classic car.

What about pets? The right kind of dog is a good idea. Do not get a chick dog like something Paris Hilton owns. You want something with character that will not scare girls away. Doberman Pinschers and Bulldogs fall into the latter category. Pugs, French Bulldogs and Golden Retrievers fall into the former category. Don't get a cat. A fair percentage of women are allergic to cats. Why risk alienating them?

Chapter Thirteen

The Friend Trap: How to Convert a Friend into a Girlfriend

At one point or another every single guy seems to finds himself hanging out with a girl who he really likes and, unfortunately, while the girl likes the guy enough to hang out with him she sees him just as a friend. Even Mr. Wonderful found himself in this sort of relationship and it did not end all that well for him either.

I was hesitant to address this issue but I am going to anyway because it is so common. I should start by saying that I do not have a definite solution. The advice I am going to give you will increase your odds of success. However, even with this advice your odds remain fairly long. The advice I give you will also allow you to get some good out of a bad situation.

Here are the dynamics of this sort of the relationship: Often the woman is in a relationship (often an on again, off again relationship) where she is not being treated very well and the result is she is spending a lot of time with her "friend" who treats her like a queen. Sometimes the girl is attracted to guys who again do not treat her very well or even meet her standards and again she ends up spending a lot of time with her "friend" who worships the ground she walks on. The girl at some level knows that you are in love with her. And when you spend time with her and fail at gaining her heart you are showing her over and over again that you do not possess The Quality. This makes it very hard for you to convert her to your girlfriend.

The first bit of advice I am going to give you is the same advice your friends, your rabbi and your chiropractor have given you, break it off. Stop calling her and stop taking her calls. Move on. You know what? You are not going to take this advice so let's just keep on going.

We're going to start by trying to make some use of this relationship. When you go out with her practice your Dating Act. If you are with her on a Tuesday and you have a second date with another women on a Wednesday try out a couple stories and tease her a bit. Think of her as a practice audience, practice being charming, funny and confident. Trust me, if you can be this way in front of her you can be this way in front of anyone.

Okay, let's see if we can give you a puncher's chance to actually convert this chick into your girlfriend. Do not tell her about *The Program* but do talk about the results. Be subtle when you do this. If you meet a nice girl and you are headed for another date ask her for a suggestion about where to go on a second date. Try to mess with her head a little. Stop calling her and stop taking her calls for a week or ten days and then give her a call. Schedule something with her and then text her at the last minute saying you can't go. Embrace your friendship with her by mentioning a couple of times what a good friend she is and shake her hand hello. Then at the end of the night make a pass at her. If you can sleep with her you will most likely change the dynamics of the relationship. However, that also is unlikely to happen. Will the above work? It might, but probably not. There is generally only one way that this type of relationship ends and that is with you nursing a broken heart. I might also suggest this strategy: Dump her now in a rather cold fashion. Call her and explain that you are not interested in seeing her anymore. Do not give some teary speech about the two of you wanting different things. Just tell her you have lost interest. Then do *The Program*. In six months, call and ask her out on a date. But my guess is that by that time you will have an amazing girlfriend who actually appreciates you, and you will not even bother to call.

I will end this chapter with a story. Once upon a time there was a thirty-year old man who lived in New York. He met a lovely brown haired Princess from the Upper East Side. On their first date he fell head over heels in love with her. The Princess hesitantly went on a second date with our hero. At the end of the date the princess proposed that the two just be friends. The man readily agreed as he was desperate to see her again. What followed was a four month relationship of sorts in which the man unsuccessfully tried to change the terms of the relationship. Eventually the Upper East Side Princess found a real boyfriend and ended the friend relationship breaking our hero's heart. After some moping, he embarked on another journey in which he mastered the art of dating.

He met another Princess from the Upper West Side who had blond hair and was beautiful in all ways and really appreciated him. However, he could never get the image of the Princess from the Upper East Side out of his head and eventually broke up with the Upper West Side Princess. A couple of months later he ran into the Upper East Side Princess and, using his newfound skills, he was able to embark on a real relationship with her. Within three weeks he grew tired of her and left her. He returned to the

Princess from the Upper West Side and the two lived happily ever after.

The moral to this story is that part of what attracts men to their female "friends" is that they are unattainable. And if you find yourself in this situation there is without a doubt a wonderful woman out there who will really appreciate you and want to be much more than just friends.

Chapter Fourteen

Lies that The Typical Guy Tells Himself that Make Him less Attractive to Women

There are a too many straight men chasing too few straight women, and therefore the deck is stacked against me.
Statistically there are about one hundred and five baby boys born for every hundred baby girls born. However, you then have to factor in the following: There are more men in jail than women. Men make up about ninety percent of the jail population. There are more men stationed overseas than women. Men make up approximately ninety percent of the military stationed away from the USA. Sadly boys due to their adventurous nature are far more likely to die young than women. And finally, the studies on the subject are murky, but they all seem to indicate the same thing, percentage wise there are far more gay men than gay women. When you take these four factors into account you can see that within any particular age range there are slightly more straight women than straight men. If you don't believe it, just take a look around. There are tons of good looking women out there. Most guys are kind of plain looking. A friend of mine once complained that when she went on the subway there were always five or six really pretty women in her subway car but almost never any good looking men. Whenever I go on the subway I am amazed to find that this is almost always the case. So the deck is not

stacked against you. It is important that you do not approach dating with a doom and gloom attitude.

Women are shallow and cruel.

You have got to stop being a hater. The above is not true. Most women are wonderful and the fact that you have been rejected in the past does not change this. Having a negative and angry attitude toward women, first and foremost, is just wrong, and second, it's really unattractive. You must cleanse yourself of any negative ideas which you may harbor about women.

Women are attracted to mean guys and not nice guys like me. I should start acting mean.

The vast majority of women want to end up with a good guy such as you. You just have to do a better job of attracting them and with *The Program* you will. Yes, a very small percentage of women do seem to end up with men who treat them cruelly and this is really sad. Why would you ever want to be one of those mean spirited guys?

When I go out, I have to get a little buzzed in order to build up the courage to approach women.

You know what is at the heart of this sort of thinking? Fear Based Behavior. You have to stop being afraid of women. And you have to stop being afraid to approach women. Approaching women is a little tricky and alcohol will make it harder not easier. Chapter Twenty discusses specific techniques for overcoming shyness and approaching women. If you consider yourself to be shy, I think you will find helpful tips in that chapter.

A woman is either attracted to me or she is not, and there is nothing I can do to change that.

There is a lot you can change. Follow *The Program* and stop acting like A Typical Guy and you will be shocked at how many women are attracted to you.

If I meet a girl and she is not that into me, I will just become her friend and eventually she will get to know me and become my girlfriend.

The truth is that she probably won't. You are better off spending your time meeting and dating new girls than dating girls who are frankly not all that into you. Part of the reason you think like this is Fear Based Behavior. You are so scared that you will not be able to find someone new that you latch on to any girl who will spend time with you. This, however, is not the case, which allows me to perfectly segue into Section Two of this book in which I am going to show you how to meet and date a lot of amazing women and without a doubt some of them will be very into you.

Section Two: Getting Dates and Dating

Chapter Fifteen
Mastering Online Dating: Part One

When I first joined *Match.com,* I read a profile in which a very pretty and slightly stuck up girl started her profile by saying that if you are not the type of guy who would approach her in a bar then don't bother writing her an email. She had an interesting point which I would like to examine.   At a bar a girl like her would only be approached by a Mr. Wonderful. The Typical Guy would look at her, certainly would think about her but would be very unlikely to approach her.

I disregarded her point and wrote to her anyway. I ended up going out with her a couple of times. In fact, I went on numerous dates with numerous girls who I never would have approached at a bar. Some of those girls I ended up dating for a while. With regards to that specific girl, if the guys approaching her at bars were so great why, while edging towards thirty, had she decided to join *Match.com?*

One of my business partners went on a trip to Spain and when I asked him what the girls were like there he said, "Joe, there were a lot of pretty girls there, but there is nothing like the girls of New York." Okay, I am a bit biased, but I had to agree. The point being is that in New York City where the single girls are absolutely stunning, almost all of them are either on or have been on *Match.com, Yahoo Dating, J date, OK cupid, More Fish in The Sea* or *EHarmony*. Do not feel the least bit stigmatized about joining. Just do it!

We are now going to go over the nuts and bolts of internet dating. For starters, join the site with the most members in your area. Most of the sites allow you to browse for free. I would take advantage of that. You are looking for are a lot female members in your age bracket who are real.

We are going to start with your profile. I would go with no less than two pictures and no more than four pictures. Avoid going shirtless or showing off your car. You want to look clean cut and well put together. If you have some pictures of you at a party and you are well dressed go with them. Pictures of you in suit or blazer are also good. Post a lot of pictures on the site and see which ones you look the best in. Then use those in your profile. I went through a large number of pictures of myself before narrowing them down to the few in which I looked the best. Your pictures are so important that you might even consider hiring a professional photographer so you can be sure of having some good shots. If you struggle with your weight definitely go with pictures of you in a suit or a blazer. As you lose weight and get in better shape in *The Program* because of the exercise and weight loss, be sure to update the pictures on your profile.

The text of your profile should be slightly humorous, smart and confident. Do not put yourself down. Make it about four paragraphs long. Mention your job in a good light but do not devote too much space to it. Most women are looking for a guy about their age up to ten or eleven years older. Use this age range as your guideline. In your profile under whom you are looking for if your are thirty-nine do not put thirty-nine to eighteen—it creeps women out. Instead, under whom you are looking for put your age to approximately ten years younger.

On *Match.com* and other dating sites when you fill out your profile you will see a place to list your favorite things and your favorite spots to hang out. Fill these sections out. You want to list familiar things that women can write to you about. List your favorite restaurant, your favorite TV show, where you have traveled, what you like to do, for example, hiking or cooking. In your profile and in these sections go easy on sports and leave out any references to science fiction and video games. The next chapter is completely devoted to setting up your profile—read it carefully.

I wish that all you need to do is to set up your profile, sit back and let the messages from woman roll in. Alas, it just does not work that way. You are going to be sending out four Opening Email messages a day, every day. An Opening Email is the initial email that you send to women whose profile has caught your eye. The women you will be approaching should be in your appropriate age range and live within approximately sixty miles of you. These Opening Emails have to be specific to each women you are writing. No cutting and pasting Opening Emails over and over. Emails should be a little on the short side, anywhere from three to seven sentences long. In the email always be confident and polite. Avoid praising her too much. Try to bring in a bit of humor. I have another chapter just devoted to emails that you will be writing that is very important. For now I am going just to sketch out the process.

When you get an email back from a girl your second email to her should be more conversational. You should write about your weekend and what you have been up to lately. Make sure you ask her questions. Again try to be funny and witty, maybe flirt a little. When you get an email back from her write her back as soon as possible. I cannot emphasize this point enough. On the third or fourth email arrange a phone conversation. In general, write an email back to a girl requesting her number after you have received a second email from her.

When you get her number call her as soon as possible. On the phone be smart and confident. Ask her questions. I would speak to her for about fifteen to twenty minutes. At the end of the conversation ask her out for a drink or on a date of some sort.

If you do this well, meaning that you read the entire book and consistently write and send strong emails, you should start getting dates within two to three weeks. This is a numbers game. I started this process twice, and both times within about ten days, I was writing back and forth to a number of women but no dates. By about day twelve I was trading phone calls with several girls. Almost to the day, fourteen days in, I had two dates set up. After the third week, just from *Match.com,* I had two to three dates a week for months on end.

Once you have met a girl you like, keep on writing and dating other women. The Typical Guy meets a girl he likes and stops pursuing other women. Mr. Wonderful keeps on dating until he is in an exclusive relationship. Remember this is one of the important lessons that we have learned from Mr. Wonderful.

A couple of key points about this chapter:

1)   Make sure you send four original Opening Emails each day. Not one, not two, not three, FOUR OPENING E-MAILS PER DAY!

2)   Always email back promptly. When you get a girl's number, call her that night. I cannot emphasize this enough.

3)   Make sure your Opening Emails are geared specifically to her. No cutting and pasting.

4)   After you have a date or you've met a girl you really like, don't stop the process. Keep sending four Opening Emails each day.

The following two chapters discuss internet dating more completely. Read them carefully. Along with this chapter, they are very important.

Chapter Sixteen

Mastering Online Dating: Part Two
How to Write the Perfect Profile

As discussed in Chapter Fifteen, your profile should be humorous, smart, and confident. The text should be around four paragraphs in length. In a lot of ways your internet profile is a reflection of what your dating personality should be and consequently the same rules apply. Your profile needs to be upbeat and charming, so obviously do not put yourself down. You want to present yourself as someone who is social, active and interesting. Mention hobbies that would likely be interesting to females. If you play a sport such as soccer, tennis or even touch football in the park, mention it. Book clubs, hiking, wine tasting, martial arts, and cooking are also all good. Science fiction, video games, online video games and anything else that screams loser geek, leave out. Again, be very selective with the pictures you choose for your profile. Make sure your profile is free of spelling errors and obvious grammatical mistakes. Run the text through Microsoft Word and check it for spelling and grammatical errors.

Regarding the text, I would write it and then have someone, preferably a friend who is good with women and has a good sense of humor, punch it up for you. I once heard how Chris Rock prepares for a comedy special. He would do his act in front of some comedian friends and then take them out to dinner and listen to their suggestions on how to improve his act. Well, if this process is good enough for Chris Rock, a similar process is good enough for your profile.

Somewhere in your profile there should include a brief description of your job and how much you like it. You should also briefly discuss what you're looking for in a relationship. Let me tell you what you are looking for in a relationship…a serious relationship, not a fling.

Mention your good points but skip your troubles. This is not the place to mention how difficult dating has been. In fact if there is one thing you learn from this book, it is to never say that to anyone at anytime. DO NOT put yourself down or make fun of yourself in your profile. When I started looking at the profiles of guys for this book, I was surprised at how so many of them made this mistake. Some of the guys seemed like they had an obligation to criticize themselves.

Another major mistake men make in their profiles is they apologize, or say how ambivalent they are about being on an internet dating site. Do not do this! You are on the site. She is on the site. Accept it and move on. Expressing ambivalence about internet dating is another form of putting yourself down, something absolutely not permitted in *The Program*. In your profile, do not tell a story that makes you look bad, again this is just another form of putting yourself down. I don't understand the reason, but when guys write their profile they tend to do this.

Your profile is also not the place for diatribes on any subject. At one point when I was doing research for this book I came across a guy's profile which was very funny and well written. In it the writer, who had just moved from

New Zealand to New York, described his first date in his new city in which the girl read his palm and told him all about his past lives. However, he ended the profile with a diatribe on atheism and how he thought religion was rather foolish. Okay, that's his opinion, and I respect that, but why ensure that the seventy percent of the women who are religious will not write you? The point is that when it comes to politics and religion in your profile: Pipe down.

The Quality really does not apply to your profile, not if you've prepared it as I've instructed. If you have, your profile tells girls that you have The Quality by presenting you as a humorous, active, smart, well dressed gentlemen, but nowhere in your profile should you mention other women.

Next I am going to review three actual profiles. My purpose is to point out their weaknesses and strengths. This process should help you write your profile.

Hank's profile: Grade F

Title: Frustrated Typical Guy

Well hello there ladies (And I suppose the occasionally slightly curious gentlemen…hey wrong section there buddy…not that there is anything wrong with that…LOL)

But I digress because rather then tell you how much I love exploring the city or hanging out with my friends I have bigger fish to fry…That is I want to address a question … A question that has beguiled men since the Stone Age…A question that has stumped the best of us….

JUST WHAT DO WOMEN WANT??????

You say you want a nice guy, someone who treats you well, someone who will listen to you, who will buy you flowers, will cook for you...and to this I have to say....Oh come on, who are we kidding?

I am twenty-nine years old and you see those foot prints all over my back? LOL those are from me being walked all over by women for being a nice guy.....LOL

I have taken you to expensive dinners...cooked you gourmet dinners (And were not talking about Chef Boy R .D here) listened to your stories, encouraged you, etc., etc., etc., and what I have gotten for it? Mistreated, dumped, turned down, dumped, told I made a really good friend (Oh the pain, the pain) and did I mention dumped?

I imagine there is club somewhere where ladies get together and laugh themselves silly over nice guys like me. "And then get this, he bought me flowers and cooked me a really great dinner all the while I bored him to death by giving him a blow by blow account of what a jerk my ex was Ha Ha Ha Ha...So then I told him he would make a really great friend and left to go hook up with my jerk of an ex...no no he broke up with my former best friend.....well they were on a break he just has not got around to telling her yet."

Okay I am not the best guy in the world... I am certainly not perfect...I may not be as rich Bill Gates or as handsome as Brad Pitt. But I think I am pretty okay looking I have been known to attend a gym and I have a decent steady job. I am kind and decent and a total gentlemen. :) I know a bit about art and culture. I have seen a movie or two with subtitles....All in all I should be a catch. :)

I am looking for someone who is kind, smart, and has a good sense of humor. It would not hurt if you were easy on the eyes. Are you out there? If you are drop me a line.

This profile is brutal. It actually stood out to me because it managed to break almost every rule I lay out in this book. Even the title is terrible: "Frustrated Typical Guy." He starts out by immediately putting himself down. The writer opens his profile with several paragraphs basically explaining how he does not understand women and how bad he is with women. This obviously is a huge mistake as he is starting out by telling women in the clearest possible terms that he does not possess The Quality. Later he states,

"I am certainly not perfect...I may not be as rich as Bill Gates or as handsome as Brad Pitt."

Hank is again putting himself down, which he should not do. The grammar and spelling in this profile are just atrocious. It would have taken Hank ten minutes to cut and paste this profile and run it through Microsoft Word to check it for spelling and grammar mistakes, but he did not bother. The result is that it looks like it was written by a sixth grader. Hank's profile is too long and thus a chore to read. Finally, Hank uses smiley face symbols and the term LOL. Girls do this all the time, which is fine because they are girls. Do not use either of these symbols and terms in your profile or for that matter, ever. As far as I can tell from this profile, Hank is a pretty funny guy. This profile with a couple of adjustments would make for a fairly funny standup comedy routine. But this sort of self-deprecating humor is terrible from a dating perspective, and a guy as funny as Hank should be able to be entertaining without putting himself down.

Jed's Profile: Grade B

Title: It's a beautiful day stop watching TV and go out and play

Hey there, how are you doing? How are you finding internet dating? That good, Huh? Well don't worry I have a feeling that things are about to start looking up.

I like to stay active. I enjoy hiking, mountain climbing, and the occasional jump off a plane. (With a parachute) I just came back from a trip with some friends in which we spent two weeks hiking and mountain climbing, in and around the Grand Canyon. If you have never been I would highly recommend it. Who knows? Maybe with me? I can't wait to go back.

When I am here in the city I like to take advantage of all that it has to offer. I like live music, (I grew up playing the guitar and I can play a bit of music myself) I have a subscription to The Museum of Modern Art which is one of my favorite places and there is nothing wrong with chilling in the back of a lounge with a dry martini.

Work wise I work as an executive for small record company which has been something of a roller coaster ride.

I am looking for someone who is down to earth and has a real sense of herself.

I will end this profile with two moments of embarrassment. When I first was learning to

Mountain climb I managed to get myself stuck on a ledge and had to be rescued by a helicopter. And once while hiking I got lost in a rather small patch of forest.

I basically spent three hours walking in a circle. (Don't worry if you go hiking with me. My sense of direction has improved and I now own a GPS watch.)

This is a pretty strong profile. It stands out a bit. He shows himself to be confident and active. The weakest part occurs when he tries to be funny. Jed should just leave out the two stories about getting stranded and lost. If he just eliminates those paragraphs Jed has himself a fairly strong profile. The profile could use a bit more humor although the opening is strong. Jed could do a slightly better job presenting his work in a better light. And somewhere in the profile Jed should indicate that he is looking for a real relationship.

Joe's Profile: Grade A

Title: Hi

Instead of using words like wonderful, charming, and down to earth to describe myself (all true by the way) I am going to cut to the chase and tell you what I am looking for.

I am looking for a real relationship, not to hook up with the hostess at an Olive Garden. No disrespect to either hostesses or the Olive Garden. (When you are here you are family.)

I'm a Cancer which means I am very outgoing. I am funny, well read and an intellectual. I know a bit about wine. I am a great cook. I like traveling to Europe and occasionally wandering aimlessly around Manhattan looking for the perfect French Bistro. Want to come?

I am a partner in a family owned real estate development firm (which means I run the show while my Dad plays golf). For me it is kind of a dream job.

Stuff I love: My nephew/God son (greatest kid ever) The Mets, (hey no one's perfect) Brunch on the Upper West Side and making my friends laugh.

I am looking for someone who is interesting, philosophical, and passionate. Has a kind spirit and is almost as charming as me.

This profile looks good. Notice that Joe has hit all high notes. Funny, check. Likes his job, check. Wants a real relationship, check. Involved in interesting activities, check. Joe also does not put himself down and his profile is free of spelling errors.

Chapter Seventeen

Mastering Online Dating: Part Three
 How to Write the Perfect Opening Emails

The Opening Emails you send out are extremely important. In *The Program* you are going to send out four Opening Emails a day every single day. In this chapter I go over with you some Opening Emails that I wrote in the past to girls I was interested in on *Match.com*. Then I look at a few good emails and explain why they were good. Finally, I include two emails that were not very good and explain why these emails were not effective. Do not take any of these emails and write them out as your own. It will not work. Every email has to be specifically written to the girl you are interested in. The chapter closes with a few tips that will help you with internet dating.

   Again, Opening Emails should be anywhere from three to seven sentences long. Always be confident and polite in the email and avoid praising the girl too much. If you can, be funny or even tease her. Before you write an email, study her profile carefully. Then write a short note based on one or two items in her profile. Be playful and you can flirt a bit. Always make the email easy to answer. It's a good idea to ask a question or two in the email. Do not put yourself down or make fun of yourself.

   When choosing someone to write to, first make sure that you can write her a pretty good Opening Email. If you feel you can't, find someone else. Before you send the email, check it for spelling errors and grammatical mistakes. Cut and paste the email into Microsoft Word, run spell check and grammar check and then cut and paste it back.

I wrote an Opening Email to Anna who wrote the following in her profile:

> Hi, how are you? Here's how I see this going down…we go out, we drink (I like my Martini's dry.) We laugh a little and if I don't like you maybe I will set you up with one of my cute friends. I am laid back and funny I can be very casual but I also like to dress up and occasionally go out some place fancy.
>
> I am looking for a genuine good guy….I am done with the crazies. I want a guy who gets it. Who is done with the clubs and going out seven nights a week. And who understands how to treat a lady.
>
> In my spare time I like shopping, antiquing, yoga and going to the movies. I like board games and I am mad good at scrabble.
>
> Are you out there? If are you are drop me a line

I wrote the following Opening Email to Anna:

> Hi, I like your profile. You seem like you are a lot of fun. I am glad to hear you are done with the crazies. Do you really like antiquing? I hope this is not a deal breaker but there is no way you can beat me in scrabble.
> Joe

This Opening Email works because it's related to the girl's profile in a specific way. It includes some gentle teasing making it slightly critical, but only a little. There's a bit of humor in it, it's short and it's easy for her to reply. You should be able to see the process I used to write it. I read her profile and used a couple items in my email.

I wrote an Opening Email to Betty who wrote the following in her profile:

> I have great friends and I love spending time with them, but it would be nice to meet a man who shares similar values and goals in life, has fun hobbies and interests. I enjoy travel (Europe is my favorite), weekend getaways and simply wandering around the city. I like reading, book clubs (I am quite the bookworm), warm summer nights and the beach. It would be nice to meet someone who is caring mature and ambitious, someone who is kind and likes to hold hands. I would love to meet someone who is adventurous, open-minded and who enjoys making other people happy.
>
> Some of my favorite places are Argentina, Prague and New England in the Fall, anywhere really with the right company.

I responded to Betty's profile with the following Opening Email:

> Hi, like you I love to read. (Traveling is fun too, have you ever been to Italy? Florence is my favorite city). My favorite book is *Catcher in the Rye*. What is yours?

This is a fairly strong Opening Email. Again it is short, specific to her profile and easy for her to reply to. I couldn't think of anything funny to say so I did not. You don't have to be absolutely brilliant in each email you write.

Jenny from Brooklyn wrote the following in her profile:

> Hi I am a twenty-eight year old girl who grew up in Brooklyn and now lives in Manhattan with my sister, who is also my best friend.
>
> Family is important to me and I definitely eventually want kids. I am looking for a real relationship If you are a player just move on to the next girl.
>
> I like guys who are smart, intellectual men. No Guidos …no guys who wear man jewelry…if you refer to girls as chicks you are probably not my type.
>
> I like to read, (I am a member of a book club) hang out with friends, go out to see the occasional live band in Brooklyn (There is no place like home) and go out to dive bars with friends. (See I am not total snob).
>
> If you like what you read write me back and say hello.

I responded to this profile with the following Opening Email:

> Hi there, I recently sold most of my man jewelry on eBay (The recession has called for drastic measures from us real estate guys) so I thought I would write to you and say hello. I think it is cool that you are in a book club. I have never been. I love to read though. What is your favorite book? Mine is *The Buddha of Suburbia.*

A buddy of mine is in a book club with the guy who wrote *The Game*. They just finished *Atlas Shrugged*. I have no idea what to make of that.

If you get the chance write me back

I gnash my teeth every time I read this email because it is so terrible. It actually got a response but nothing beyond that. The opening line was an attempt at humor, but what I was doing by making this joke was actually putting myself down by saying that real estate guys like me were now broke. In the last two sentences of the email I compounded the problem by making fun of myself. This email is also unfocused and too long. Don't send an Opening Email like this.

Amy from Manhattan wrote the following in her profile:

I am a little bit country and a little bit rock and roll.

Let me start by saying I love taking advantage of the city. And I am always up for trying a new restaurant, hanging out with my friends at a dive bar, hanging out at rock club (Which is my favorite) or dressing up and going out to someplace fancy (I clean up real nice)

And while I also love the city sometimes on the weekends I can't wait to leave. I grew up in the country and I am at times very much a country girl. I love hiking, camping and even fishing.

It would nice to meet a man who is kind, funny and gentlemen and wasn't only interested in getting in my pants. Ideally his career would be important to him but not take over his life. It would also be important to him that family is as important to him as it is me.

If this sounds like you write and say Hi

I responded to this profile with the following message:

Hi. I like your profile. You seem really pretty, special and down to earth and the type of girl I would love to meet so I thought I would write and say hello. I have something of an arts background—my parents being hippies—I was sent to an arts school where I learned to sing, paint and eventually even read. (It was actually a really amazing experience) I work in a family owned real estate business which has been crazy fun, terrifying and rewarding. I love living in the city and taking advantage of all it has to offer. My friends and family are really important to me and I have known most of my friends since childhood. I am smart, kind-hearted and definitely a gentleman.

If you get the chance write me back.

This Opening Email fails for a number of reasons. I start off by praising her way too much thus exhibiting Fear Based Behavior. Maybe you think it looks like a cut and paste job which I sent out over and over. Maybe that's because it is a cut and paste job which I sent out over and over. Because of this, it does not relate to her profile. Do not do this. Every Opening Email has to be tailored to an individual. As if that's not enough, this email has other problems. It's way too long and therefore it's a bit of chore to slog through. It is kind of a life history or a resume.

What you want to do is write something to her that will convince her respond, not tell her your life story. The spelling and grammar in this email are sloppy. That's bad because it produces a bad impression. Spell and grammar check every email before you send it. The last flaw is that I didn't even make it easy to reply to.

While cutting and pasting is absolutely forbidden you can and should reuse lines that have worked in previous Opening Emails. Never forget, though, that the reused line must relate to the girl's profile.

Jenny wrote in her profile:

> Hi my name is Jenny I am an artist who studied fine art in London and I now work for an art gallery on the Upper East Side which is kind of a dream job for me.
>
> I also paint in my spare time. I live with my two best friends on the lower east side and the world's greatest Mutt. I love hanging out in the village, going to museums and definitely going out to see live bands. I am really into music my dogs name is Bono LOL (Guess who my favorite band is?)
>
> I am looking for a nice guy who has similar interests.

I wrote the following Opening Email to Jenny:

> Like you, I have something of an arts background. My parents being hippies, I was sent to an arts school where I learned to sing, paint, act and eventually even read. And even though I did not go that way work wise (I am a very creative real estate developer) I think it

was an incredible experience which still shapes me today.

Have you been to any cool music shows lately? I just attended a concert that a friend of mine gave in the park which was a lot of fun.
Joe

Notice that I did reuse a line, but it matched perfectly with Jenny's profile. It's a reasonably strong line. This Opening Email, while not the greatest, is pretty strong, and it got a response.

To close this chapter, I want to show how this email conversation played out to completion. Jenny wrote the following email back to me:

Hi Joe, it was nice to hear back from you...It's funny, I just attended an outdoor concert in the park. I saw a jazz band LPD. Was that your friend's band? By the way I used to work as a hostess at The Olive Garden
:).
Jenny

Hi Jenny, Oh No! Not another hostess from the Olive Garden, I can't seem to walk past that place without a hostess running after me with her number...That is really cool that you saw LPD in the park (Not my friend's band though, which is too bad I really like them) I wanted to go but I was at the Jersey Shore for a long weekend. Have you managed to take any time off this summer?
Joe

Hi Joe,

The Jersey Shore sounds like fun. I am planning to go visit my family there next weekend at my Mom's house in Orchid Park. Where was your friend's house? No trips this summer so far but I do have a three week trip to Barcelona planned for late July. I can't wait.

Jenny

Hi Jenny,

I am kind of jealous. I was in Barcelona last summer at a wedding and it was just amazing. Do you want to talk on the phone sometime? My number is 917 568 **** or e-mail me your number and I will give you a call.

Joe

Sure it would be nice to chat my number is 917 676 **** I am around tonight around 7 P.M.. Look forward to talking to you :).

Jenny

I would then call her the next night. What you can see from this email dialogue is that the tone is mostly conversational. If I could I would try to be funny and flirt a bit which I tried to do with her joke about working as a hostess at an Olive Garden. But in the back and forth it's mostly conversational. When I received the second email from Jenny, I wrote and asked for her number. This is about the correct timing. When you ask to talk to her do not ask her out rather say you would like to speak to her as you do not want to get too far ahead of yourself. Always make sure that you ask her for her number. I would usually also give the girl my number when I asked for hers but I was just being polite. My real intention was always that I would call her.

When you get her number call her as soon as possible. On the phone be smart and confident. Ask her questions. I would speak to her for about fifteen to twenty minutes. At the end of the conversation ask her out for a drink or on a date of some sort.

As you write more Opening Emails, you get better at it. In the beginning it will probably take you about an hour to write your daily quota of four Opening Emails per day. Two or three weeks into *The Program* should see this down to about a half hour. In the beginning of *The Program* I would say your response rate to Opening Emails is about one in eight. Do not get discouraged because you are writing twenty-eight Opening Emails a week because over time, this should yield two to three dates a week. Remember, it does take about two weeks before you actually start going on dates. With experience your response rate will improve.

More Tips for internet dating:

 You can expect to have a situation where you write a girl, she writes you back, but then after you write her back, the two of you lose touch. This happens often. What I did was to wait about a month and then drop her line. I start by mentioning that we'd written back and forth again but then lost touch. I was careful not mention that she'd been the one who stopped writing so as not to put myself down. Quite often, this resulted in a response.

Patience is a virtue. If a girl writes you back, write her again immediately. However, if she takes her time writing you back don't worry about it. Sometimes the pace with dating can be fairly slow. Just make sure it is slow on her end and not yours.

There is usually a spot where you could see who looked at your profile. If a girl looks at your profile, definitely write her. I would usually start by saying something like, "I noticed you were checking me out and you seem really cool, and I thought I would say hello." Then write a strong Opening Email. These Opening Emails tend to get a fairly high percentage response rate.

When you write your four Opening Emails on Sunday, send them out earlier in the day. I noticed that a lot of women would log in and respond to emails written to them early Sunday night. Opening Emails written in the morning on Sunday got a better response rate.

Write some Opening Emails to women whose profiles do not have pictures on them. Again your response rate will improve. A girl whose profile did not have a picture winked at me and I responded with an email. We wrote back and forth a couple times and then met for a date. At one point she even commented to me that I was rather brave to agree to go out with her without seeing her picture. She actually turned out to be one of the prettiest girls I have ever seen.

If you are interested in a girl on *Match.com* never ever wink. Be a man and write her an Opening Email. Winking just makes you look like a total and complete loser.

Occasionally you will get an email or wink from a woman who read your profile. Be sure to always email her back quickly. I found that if a woman initiated contact with me almost always resulted in a date.

Do not view a woman's profile over and over. Usually she can see who is viewing her profile and looking at her profile over and over indicates to her that you do not have

The Quality. If you like her profile view it once and then write to her immediately.

On *Match.com* you can favor a women's profile. Don't do this. She can see that you favored her and again it indicates to her that you do not have The Quality. On the other hand, if you see a girl has favored you write her immediately.

In a women's profile there is usually an indication of whether she has been actively using the dating site. Generally you want to write women who have been using the site within the last twenty-four hours or in the last few days. This is important because these women are more likely to respond to you. If you see a women's profile that you really like but it indicates that she has not been active on the dating web site, write down her profile name and every once in a while check out her profile. If you see she has become active again, write her immediately.

With regards to your profile, it should always be a work in progress, that is, always figure on devoting a bit of time to trying to improve it. At one point I changed my profile headline to a line from a John Bon Jovi song where he sings about his guitar and playing from the heart. I don't know why but I thought the line had a nice ring to it. Well, it didn't and my response rate went down a bit over the next couple of weeks. I then switched the headline to "This is where the beautiful people live" and the response rate went up. I have no idea why. The point is that sometimes you just have to experiment a bit.

Writing an Opening Email and receiving no response does not necessarily mean that it was a bad Opening Email. You really have no idea why you didn't get a response. It's also true that on occasion, you will find that you write a bad Opening Email and receive a response.

Don't be afraid to experiment a bit with your Opening Emails. Doing so will probably result in you writing the occasional bad Opening Email. So what? It also will lead to you into writing more innovative Opening Emails.

Chapter Eighteen

How To Find and Succeed at Singles Events

What I liked about single events was there was a more level playing field. A girl just by being there is indicating that she is looking for someone. The dreaded words "I have a boyfriend" are rarely heard. I want you to hit two singles events a week. There are plenty of them out there and you will never find which ones work for you unless you start exploring them. I define singles events in a broad way, and there are tons of them out there. A good place to start looking is the *Craigslist's* events and classes section. Another great resource is *meetup.com*. A third area is churches or other religious institutions. The Catholic Church tends to sponsor an after-Mass Sunday afternoon get together for singles, usually at a local pub. I would definitely check it out even if you are not Catholic. Museums often also sponsor a singles night. Swing dancing and speed dating events also are worth trying out. Other venues include dance classes, wine tasting, booze cruises, bar crawls and even bar trivia and game nights.

Every Sunday night I would go on the internet and find two singles events to attend for the upcoming week. This was not that big a deal but I was persistent with it. No rest for the weary. Some events were an utter waste of time and some of them yielded dates. What really mattered, however, was that I was out there in an environment with a lot of women who are also looking for dates, and I was trying new things to find out what would work.

Find an event that works for you. Of course, this might take some time. So what? Single types of events tend to be pretty affordable. They often are free and usually the bars that hold them tend to offer specials. One the first events I attended was a singles poker night at the local Jewish Cultural Center (On the Upper West Side of Manhattan—a JCC is somewhat like a YMCA.) There were not any girls there and most of guys there were in college but I still had good time, learned a bit about poker (mostly that it bored me to tears) and chalked it up to experience. The next event that I attended was a lecture series given at a local bar in Manhattan that was geared toward singles that was sponsored by the Catholic Church. I am actually Roman Catholic so attending this event made sense but again this event did not really work for me. A friend of mine had a lot success with swing dancing. He took some classes aimed at singles and then found some events. For him it was a great way to meet girls and get dates. I tried it out and learned that I was a horrible dancer. It was not really my thing. Eventually, I struck upon art events geared toward singles, a bar trivia night and book clubs as events that yielded dates.

However, I do not know what will work for you. The only way for you to find out if a particular event will work is to try it. You might find that a Catholic lecture night is a great place to find dates and that a book club is totally not your thing. Find singles events and get out there, try them and get dates.

Next, we need to cover some strategies for succeeding at these events. Dress sharply, since you are planning this event in advance this should not be a problem. You should either return home and change into a date outfit or bring the outfit to work and then wash up and change before you leave. Remember the principles of *The Program*. If I were you the night before the event, I would reread Chapter Six on Improving Your Dating Personality.

Do not spend too much time at the event. Get there and be social. Hold yourself with confidence, be upbeat, funny, and charming. Do no put yourself down. If you meet a girl after a lecture, chat with her about it, ask questions and pay attention. If you're shy and this sounds impossible, have heart. Chapter Twenty is about approaching women and overcoming shyness, which also should help you at singles events.

Whatever event you attend, try to be knowledgeable. If you are at a singles wine tasting event, find out what wines you will be drinking in advance (do a little research on it.) However, make sure not to bore a girl to death with a ten minute dissertation on the aging process of Tuscan wines but rather to be interesting and knowledgeable about the subject before moving the conversation elsewhere.

You have to force yourself to be a little aggressive about approaching and talking to people at these events. The worst thing you can do is to stare into space. (Obviously, this illustrates that you do not possess The Quality.) I want you to work the room a bit. Talk to both men and women in short conversations. At a mixer type event give yourself thirty-five to forty-five minutes. This makes it a bit easier to constantly stay social. Limit yourself to one drink. You want to be at your sharpest.

I will now introduce the concept of "Working the Room." That is when you attend a singles event or other social event, introduce yourself and chat with both men and women. Strike up conservation with a girl, chat with her for a bit and then politely move on to the next person. The very nature of these events makes it pretty easy to approach someone as most of the people there do not know any of the other attendees, and they are specifically looking to meet new people. No one likes to be in a group staring into space alone so in a sense by approaching someone you are doing her a favor. In addition, at a singles event you almost always have an opening topic of conversation, which is "Have you ever been to this event before?"

Give yourself a quota that you will approach and talk to several girls and that you will ask at least one girl for her number. If you chat with a girl that you like, speak to her for a couple minutes and then politely move on to someone else. However, while you are talking to her, always give her your full attention. Politely move on and chat with other people for fifteen minutes, and then approach her again. Tell her you have to leave shortly, tell you are meeting some friends for a party or whatever then ask her for her number. What you are doing is making yourself a limited quantity. By talking to several girls and then asking only one for her number, you are selecting her, which sends out the signal that you have The Quality. Following this approach increases the odds that she will give you her number.

What I have discussed in this chapter so far is not rocket science. What it comes down to is that you should work to find events where your strength lies and where there are available women to approach. I am also telling you that when you attend these events you should be aggressive, social, well dressed, charming, confident, smart, upbeat and to Work the Room in order to convey that you have The Quality. That said, you will be shocked how effective this will be.

Speed Dating

Speed dating is an organized event where men and women get together and move from table to table, each spending about eight minutes together on a "date". At the end of the night, every one returns home, goes on the internet and chooses who they would like to see again. If both the guy and the girl select each other their email addresses are exchanged. While this format has its drawbacks, I would definitely add a speed dating event into your rotation of singles events. The upside of these events is you approach approximately eight single women and effectively ask them out.

At speed dating events there is usually a period before the event where everyone is just hanging around the bar. Strike up a conversation with a girl during this period. I found this to be very hard to do. I understand that. I had to force myself, but it is important. One of the things we talk about in this book is that it is important to establish that you are good with women. If you spend the time just staring into space feeling uncomfortable, it will be noticed and remembered. Be social and friendly. Sometimes when you attend these events you find that the guys and girls are all bunched up on opposite sides of the bar making it kind of tough to approach a girl to strike up a conversation. Again you want to appear social and outgoing. Do not be a wall flower!

When you do go on a mini date at a speed dating event, much of what we discussed in Chapter Six applies.

Be funny, upbeat and charming. Do not drink too much and remember your manners. Keep in mind that the more you practice improving your dating personality the better you get at it.

If the two of you connect when you get her email address write her an email immediately. The email should have a conversational tone and it should be about a paragraph long. At the end of the email say that it would be nice if you could speak to her and ask for her number. Do not ask her out in the email. This email should look something like the following:

Hi Belinda, I met you at the speed dating event. How was your weekend? Did you have fun on Friday? I had a good time although it is kind of a blur. It was really nice meeting you though. Would you like to talk on the phone sometime? Could you email me your number?
Joe

After she gives you her number, call her back as soon as possible, speak to her for about twenty minutes and then ask her out.

Chapter Nineteen

Parties, Bars, Trains, Planes and Other Ideas

Parties

Parties are great places to meet women. The first step of course is to get invited to parties. Getting invitations to parties is something that can be worked at. Just by being social and staying in touch with friends generally leads to a couple of party invitations. Also try joining groups and volunteer groups. Becoming involved in such groups often leads to invitations to parties.

Once you are at a party use the strategies laid out previously for singles events. Get there and be social. Work the Room: talk to girls and guys. Again you want to give the vibe that you have The Quality. Hold yourself with confidence, be upbeat, funny, and charming. Do no put yourself down. Introduce yourself to new people. If you meet a girl you are interested in, chat with her a couple of times, do not be clingy and sometime near the end of the night ask her for her number.

I actually found that I worked much better at parties where I did not know many people. With *The Program* you force yourself into becoming a guy who feels comfortable approaching and chatting with new people. I found that at parties with people I had known for years, I would fall in to the old habit of putting myself down. This does not mean you should stop attending parties where you know people.

Instead, it means that you have to be vigilant about not falling into old habits.

Bars

I am not huge fan of bars, but the fact is most single guys are going to spend a certain amount of time in bars with an eye toward meeting women so you may as well make the best of it. The same rules that apply to single events and parties apply to bars. Remember what I wrote about limiting your time in any particular bar. Do not drink too much. In fact you might consider volunteering as the designated driver for your friends and not drinking at all.

Trains, planes and busses

When you board a train, scan the seats and sit next to a pretty girl. Then ignore her while you read a magazine or check your email on your phone. After ten minutes, strike up a conversation with her. Before she leaves ask for her number. The odds are that unless she gives you her number you are never going to see her again so you have nothing to lose. This strategy should work on busses and planes as well.

Vacations

Traveling offers a great opportunity to meet women. Women on vacation tend to be very open towards meeting guys. There are plenty of vacation packages and cruises that are geared towards singles. Since you are probably going to spend time and money on vacations anyway, why not use them as opportunities to meet women?

When you set up a vacation do a bit of research. There are web sites that offer reviews of vacation packages and cruises. You want to make sure that the place offers a nice atmosphere for meeting women and that it has a favorable ratio of men to women. Sometimes customer's reviews leave an email address. You might contact a couple of the reviewers and ask them a few of questions about the vacation that you are considering attending. You can also call or email the company that runs the cruise or vacation destination and ask them a couple of questions.

A friend mine went on a single oriented cruise to Spain during the off-season. That surprised me because he made a very good living. He told me he chose the timing of the trip because he discovered through a bit of research that more women chose that time of year to travel. He said he had a pretty great trip.

There is no problem with going on one of these trips alone, however, if you can convince a single friend to go along with you, all the better. Also a lot of these trips will have a "reunion" night at a bar a couple of weeks after the vacation has ended. Make a point to attend such an event.

Set up your single friends

You might meet some of your single guy friends and see if you can hook them up with any of your single girl friends. The idea being that they will also try to set up their single friends with you. This is an idea worth exploring.

Making friends with women

You should not make friends with single girls with the intention of eventually converting them to your girlfriend. We have already covered the problems with doing this. If you make friends with women, do so without ulterior motives. Where is it written that you can only have male friends? Make friends with women. Obviously hanging out with women will open up more opportunities to meeting other women who will be potential girlfriends.

Politics

Politics offers great opportunities to meet women. In election and primary season which make up a fair amount of time there are plenty of opportunities to volunteer for all sorts of campaigns. You should look into this. Women tend to be Democrats, I would recommend you therefore get involved with Democrat politics. My personal politics lean (slightly) center-left, but that's unimportant. If women favored the Republican Party, which in some parts of the country is the case, I would be telling you to volunteer for Republican candidates. You should also check out the Young Republican organization and The Young Democrat organization in your area. These organizations are also great places to meet women. Keep in mind your reason for getting involved in politics, to meet women, not to get some candidate elected.

Chapter Twenty

How to Overcome Shyness and Approach Women

Most of my work as an adult has involved sales and marketing. In my twenties I worked for a high end construction company mostly marketing expensive renovations to wealthy Manhattan condo owners. I would meet with owners and pitch them about our company. The process did not intimidate me at all. Later when I started working in real estate marketing I rather routinely would cold call landlords and try to convince them to list the apartments with the company I was representing. A lot of people find cold calling to be as much fun as pulling teeth, but it did not intimate me in the least. Yet until I started *The Program,* I had a lot of trouble approaching women. Going up to a girl in a bar and asking for her number scared me to death. I eventually learned how to get over this fear, and in this chapter I am going to go over ways in which you can get over this fear as well.

Change the way you think about approaching women

When you approach a woman do not fret about whether you will succeed or fail. Be casual about it. Do not worry about it. The sun will rise and set whether she is into you or not. In *The Program* you are writing out four Opening Emails a night, and you are attending one or two singles event a week. Combining this with your internet dating and you are approaching approximately thirty women a week. If the girl you approach at a bar or singles event is not in to you, so what? One down, twenty nine to go.

Just by approaching a woman you have already won. A large portion of *The Program* is about numbers. By approaching a woman you just increased your odds. When you approach a women, what is the worst thing that can happen? She may not be into you and not give you her number. If you don't approach her what is guaranteed to happen? She will not give you her number. Just by approaching her you have succeeded. Why? Because you are giving yourself a chance to succeed.

The more you approach women the better you will get at it. Which means if you approach fifty women and all fifty react negatively, you are still ahead of the game. How? Because at the end the day what you just did was practice approaching women.

The more you work at *The Program* the better you will get at approaching women. Why? Remember the old adage that the more you practice something, the better you get at doing it? That's the way it is with *The Program* where you are constantly working to improve the way you look, the way you speak and your confidence. All of this in the long run will improve your odds when you approach a woman.

When you approach a woman keep the good work you have done with *The Program* in mind and be confident

In school if you paid attention in class and studied for the test, would you be afraid to take the test? Probably not.

Well, when you are working on *The Program,* you are in sense doing everything to pass the test of attracting women. When you approach a women carry this work with you and be confident.

With *The Program* you are often approaching women at singles events. Simply being at such events and approaching women improves your odds of success. If you are at a bar the woman you approach could be there just to hang out with her friends or she could have a boyfriend. But at a singles event, she is there to meet a guy, which means there is a chance she is looking for you.

When you approach a women keep it simple and just do it

At one point I was standing at a bar on the Upper East Side with Mr. Wonderful. A girl who had caught my eye was nearby with a few friends. I stood there waiting for the perfect moment to approach her but in reality I was putting off approaching her. I kept waiting but soon Mr. Wonderful tired of waiting on me. He walked up to the group of women, introduced himself and me and started a conversation. It was that simple. He did not wait for something brilliant to say or for the right song to play on the jukebox. He just started talking.

When you see someone you like, approach her, do not prognosticate. Stay in the moment, be confident and keep it simple.

Practice being out going and making conversation

Practice striking up conversations and being outgoing in your day-to-day life, chat with the delivery guy, the receptionist, the women at the coffee bar who makes you an espresso. Practice making small talk when there is nothing on the line. The dynamics of this and approaching a woman at a bar and speaking to her are the same. In both cases you are speaking to someone new, showing interest in them and trying to be pleasant.

Try to find singles events that make it easier to approach women
If you go to a speed dating event you are going to approach seven or more women no matter what. It is built into the event. If you go to a group dance class you are going to alternate dancing with a bunch of women. If you find approaching women to be hard, go to these types of that make it as easy as possible.

Other thoughts on this subject:
One idea that I would recommend is finding a friend who is also single and going to single events and other places with an eye towards approaching women. Having a wingman is a good approach and it often makes women easier to approach.

There really is no downside to approaching a woman. Somewhere in the back of your mind you are afraid that a woman will think less of you for approaching her. No, she is going to think that you are a single guy who is attracted to women. This is in fact the truth. Certainly you have nothing to be ashamed of for being attracted to women.

The more you approach women the easier it will get. This is because approaching women is like anything else: The more you do it the easier it gets. Which means, in the beginning of *The Program* you may just have to grit your teeth, smile and force yourself to approach a women. DON'T WORRY, IT WILL GET EASIER!

If you are shy, you no doubt fear rejection when you approach a woman. That's natural because rejection is not pleasant, but don't let it worry you. There are ways to deal with rejection, and in the next chapter I am going to show exactly how to do that.

Chapter Twenty-One

Rejection Sucks—Get Over It

Not so long ago, Mr. Wonderful, three other single friends and I would spend Tuesday nights doing volunteer work in New York. There was a single girl there who was also a volunteer, serving coffee during break time and she was an absolutely stunning blonde with a sexy English accent. While she was serving coffee to the five of us, Mr. Wonderful flirted with her a little and then asked her out. He got shot down, and we all helped out by making fun of him. Mr. Wonderful just laughed along with us. A week later he chatted with the girl again, and again asked her out. Once more the girl turned him down and once more we made fun of him. The third week the girl actually agreed to go out with Mr. Wonderful and the two ended up in a relationship. I can guarantee all five of us wanted to go out with this girl yet only Mr. Wonderful had the guts to approach her. But the real lesson here is how he reacted when he got turned down. Instead of letting it affect him, he just shrugged it off, and even laughed about it. Mr. Wonderful understood that rejection is part of the game.

I wish I didn't have to tell you this, and there is no way to sugar coat it: Rejection sucks and you are going to get rejected a lot. In fact, because you are going to be approaching a lot more girls in *The Program,* you are going to get rejected even more than before. (You are also going to have more success with women then you ever have had in your life). You just have to learn to accept rejection and move on. If you are going out with someone and they reject you, be a gentlemen and tell her you had a great time and wish her luck. I got to be pretty good at this, but inwardly I felt like someone was ripping out my heart with a shovel. I even felt this way when I was getting rejected by girls I was not all that into. You know what? I just had to learn to get over it. You have to do the same. Know that it's going to happen, prepare for it and move on to the next girl.

If you've been out with a girl a couple times and she breaks up with you when you go home, don't mope. Force yourself to work a bit on *The Program*. Send some emails, schedule a singles event, or whatever, and just get your head back in the game. The Typical Guy gets rejected and wastes some time feeling sorry for himself. Mr. Wonderful shrugs his shoulders and goes back to pursuing girls.

When I was about a month into *The Program* I got a second date with someone I really liked and I was pretty pumped about it. At the end of the date she told me she did not see a future for us. I felt pretty down in the dumps about it, but you know what made me feel much better? The fact that I had three dates lined up with three equally wonderful girls.

When you follow *The Program*, as time goes on, you will also find that you're starting to do a fair amount of rejecting yourself. I quickly discovered that I hated rejecting people about as much as I hated being rejected. If you have to reject someone, be a man about it. Call her up and tell her you think she is wonderful, but you do not think she is right for you. This whole process is no walk in the park for her either. When you reject someone you should offer to be her friend. Whether this offer is as brutal for women as it is for men, I really don't know.

I was once walking down the street with my sister. Her cell phone rang and she let it go to voicemail. She told me, "That's the guy I met last night at a club. I gave him my number but I am not that interested in him. I definitely will not go out with him."

A minute later she checked the message that he left for her. She then called him up and agreed to go on a date with him. I asked her why she changed her mind. She explained that he was "super charming" on his voice message and he came off as a "real gentlemen." You know, I think I could write a book on this story alone. I am telling you this story here to illustrate just how random dating can be and how foolish it is for you to feel bad about rejection.

This story also illustrates the importance of leaving good voicemails.

Chapter Twenty-Two

Seventeen Great Ideas for Dates

The two most common dates are either meeting for drinks or going to dinner. Almost by default in *The Program* you are going to go on quite a few of these types of dates. And while I definitely encourage you to try other ideas for dating there is nothing inherently wrong with either of these options.

Often with first dates the most pressing priority is getting the date and therefore, it is often important to just make it as convenient as possible for your potential date. I would often try to pick a place near where the girl works or lives. However, even then I would do some research. Sometimes I would call or text a friend and ask for a suggestion. Obviously, when it comes to researching upcoming dates the internet is a huge resource. Googling bars or restaurants in the neighborhood that I was interested in would often bring up great suggestions. If I found a place I liked I would see if I could get more information. I found *Yelp.com, Citysearch.com* and *Menupages.com* all to be very helpful. All three websites featured customer reviews and often through Google or the actual bar's or restaurant's website, I could see pictures of the place, which was helpful. What you are looking for in a bar is a good atmosphere, a place that is not too crowded and a place where the music does not play too loud so that you can talk. I also think meeting at a coffee bar for a cup of coffee is sometimes a better option than meeting at a bar for a drink. Again pick a place with a good atmosphere.

With regards to restaurants pick a nice place with a good atmosphere where there is a good comfort level. Do not pick a place that is extravagant and wildly expensive. When you're on a date, the girl is judging you, not the restaurant.

About half the time, simply out of convenience, a first date ends up being either dinner or a drink. However, I found that often by being imaginative, you can create a better dating experience. When you date someone you should strive to create an experience that has a bit of an adventurous feel. Here are seventeen ideas for dates that you should consider trying.

Little Italy

Invite a girl out for a walk in little Italy. And then end the date by taking her to a café for espresso and dessert.

Go out for dessert

Take a girl out for dessert at a café or a bakery that has seating. This sort of date is a little shorter than a dinner date. I found dessert shops and cafes offers a fairly date friendly and romantic atmosphere. A plus is that every one likes sweets.

Yoga

If you are into this, invite her to a yoga class. If you are good at yoga this makes for a pretty good date. If she is not that experienced, you probably want to choose a beginner's class. Afterward stop at a place nearby and get a drink or a cup of coffee with her. In the summer, various groups often do Yoga in the park which is a pretty good idea for a date as well.

Sporting events

I also found that sporting events made for a decent date activity. I know that this somewhat clashes with the line of thought that women do not like sports; however, in a lot of ways a sporting event is as much about the festive atmosphere as they are about the actual sport. What I liked about sporting events was that they are almost perfect in that you can hold a conversation or just watch the game. One drawback to sports events, particularly baseball, is they tend to be on the long side. I would recommend that you solve this problem by scheduling the date a couple innings or half a quarter into the game. When it comes to sports events it pays to do a little research. You do not have to order the most expensive seats, in fact I would encourage you not to. If you do a little research, sometimes you can find seats that are interesting and have a cool feel to them without paying too much. Most teams have websites where you can actually see the view of a game from any particular seat. The other bit of research you should do on the stadium is to find out if a particular area of the stadium has really cool food stands that serves something special. The idea is to do anything you can do to improve the date.

Museums

Museums are also a good place for a date. I love this idea for a first date and particularly for a first date with a girl who you met on internet dating. Knowing a bit about art makes you seem very cool and sophisticated. Walking around the exhibits gives you something that you can easily talk about. Again, do a little research on what you will be seeing at the museum. A little knowledge is impressive. You should also check online to see if any museums in your area are doing any social events. Some museums, in an effort to draw a younger audience, will have cocktail nights. This is another great idea for a date.

Ice cream

Meet for ice cream cones and then walk around the park or a cool neighborhood. This is something fun to do that has a laid back feel and it does not scream DATE.

Do something touristy

One of the jokes that those of us who live in New York City have is that the only time that we visit the Statue of Liberty or walk the Brooklyn Bridge is when out-of-towners visit. You might even consider taking her to a Planet Hollywood or the Hard Rock Café if you have one in your area. If the two of you are running low on conversation you can always make fun of the tourists.

Meet for a happy hour after work

Yes I know this is basically a variation on meeting a girl for a drink but there is something very festive about a good happy hour. Admittedly you may drink a little more then I recommend at this event but maybe this is one place where you bend the rules a bit. You can find websites that are devoted to providing information on happy hours. In New York City *drinkdeal.com* is well worth visiting.

Summer events, outdoor concerts in the park and films in the park

In some ways I think these events make for the perfect date. A friend mine who manages rock bands invited me to a free outdoor concert in Soho sponsored by a wine company because one of his bands had been hired to do the event. When I found out the event was being held weekly throughout the summer my eyes lit up. It was a perfect event for a date. At these events the music is somewhat in the background so you can hang out and talk or watch the band. Usually drinks are served at such events. If so, just bring a blanket, but if not, bring a bottle of wine, a bottle opener and maybe even a box of cookies.

The hot ticket or event

Every once in a while you get tickets to an opening night of a play or a very in demand concert. When you do, use it as an opportunity for a date. It will make you appear cool and cutting edge.

A great unknown singer or band

The cities are swarming with great performers who have not hit the big time yet. This makes for a fun date, if you can pick a music bar or a lounge that has cool jazzy feel, all the better.

Meet for a drink at a piano bar

These are bars in which a piano player sings and plays songs on the piano and the audience usually sings along. Such places are a lot of fun. They usually are gay bars but they tend to draw a lot of straights too.

Miniature golf

This makes for a pretty good date as there is plenty of opportunity to talk and the games do not last too long. Remember you should win the game as it is important to display Leadership.

Invite a girl over to your place and cook her dinner

This is especially good option if you have a nice place. Cooking is not that hard. Learn to cook one good dish, buy a nice bottle of wine, and some ice cream for dessert. Finish the dinner while she is arriving. Pour her a glass of wine and chat with her. This makes for a nice date and it shows her you doing something well.

Invite a girl out for a picnic in the park

Pack a picnic basket with good food and a bottle of wine and then bring her to a nice spot in the park. This is fun and relaxed. Afterwards you can walk around the park a little.

When you start dating two to three times a week you have the opportunity to try new date ideas and to develop a couple of dates that you can use over and over. As we've already discussed, the best way to get good at dating is to go on a lot of dates.

Chapter Twenty Three

The Review Process

A friend of mine once told me a story about a period in his life which lasted for a couple of weeks in which he was dating a girl casually and without much success. He said he would occasionally look at her as if she were a puzzle or a math problem which he had no clue on how to solve. If this book had been available, he would have been able to solve the equation.

In the second chapter of this book we discussed a situation where you take out a girl, she seems to have a great time, you talk about future plans and then you call the next day to ask her out again but she turns you down. You ask yourself "What went wrong?" She seemed to have a good time. She seemed to really like you. The answer is she did have a good time and she did like you but she was not attracted to you. And you probably made some mistakes. One of the best things about *The Program* is you can now figure out what you did wrong and work to not make the same mistakes on your next date.

After each date I went out on, whether I was going to go out with the girl again or not, I would review in my mind what happened on the date. What did I do right? Which stories got a good reaction and which stories landed with a thud? What did I do wrong? Was I self confident enough? Did I put myself down? The point of this review was not to beat myself up, but to improve my dating skills. How could I make the next date I went out on even better? Mr. Wonderful once told me a story of being set up on a blind date and actually meeting the wrong girl and spending one hour with her before they both realized they were standing up their expected blind dates. He gave the girl his number but he was disappointed when she didn't call him back. He later speculated that he had mentioned to her that he was at the time going through financial difficulties and he also mentioned that it was a mistake to give a girl your phone number, he should have asked for hers instead. The point is Mr. Wonderful reflected on and reviewed his dates so he could see if he made any mistakes. What's good enough for Mr. Wonderful should be good enough for you, so you need to review each date.

Every interaction you have with a woman should be examined so you can see what you were doing right and what you need to improve. When it comes to putting The Program into practice, you will make mistakes—that's fine. What's important is that you recognize your mistakes and correct them. The Review Process does not just apply to dates but to every aspect and stage of dating.

I noticed that when I left a message on a girl's voicemail, I was not at my sharpest. I tended to stutter and speak haltingly. After each message I left I would go over in my mind what I said and how I could leave a better message the next time. The same Review Process applied to actual conversations on the phone. What did I say that got a good reaction? What did I say that did not? Was the phone conversation the proper length of time? Did I speak with confidence?

The same Review Process was applied to single events and parties. How was my approach? Did I hold myself with confidence? Did I do a good enough job working the room? When it comes to internet dating, when you write a girl and get a response the first thing you should do is write her back. The second thing you should do is look at the opening email you sent her so you can reflect on why it worked.

This Review Process should not be over critical. You should also constantly be reminding yourself what you did right and what improvements you have been making. Nor should this Review Process hamper innovation. Do not be afraid to experiment with new ideas. Even when a story or a joke falls flat you should examine it and consider tweaking it and retrying it on another date. I would often review emails that I sent and conclude that they were not very strong; however, sometimes incorporated into these emails were some good lines that I would include in future emails.

Before you go on a date or talk to a girl on the phone take a moment and go over what you have been doing right lately. Also go over any recent mistakes and resolve to be aware not to repeat them. This Review Process will help you immeasurably. The more you date and review your dating behavior, the better you will get at dating.

You should also take some time each week to examine what your overall weaknesses are and see what you can do to improve those weaknesses. As you get further into *The Program* you will find that the overall changes you need to make will become far clearer. You might find that you've been a little on the annoying side. Maybe the jokes you told were on the inappropriate side. I found that I had to be extra vigilant to avoid putting myself down and work extra hard to project an image of confidence. Whatever your weaknesses are, be vigilant about identifying them and correcting them.

Don't be afraid to experiment. Switch the stories and jokes in your Dating Act. Try a new place or a new type of date. Make a pass at a girl a little earlier than you usually do. One of the points of going on so many dates in *The Program* is to find out what works for you.

Chapter Twenty-Four

The Gray Area

As you work your way through *The Program* you are going to make some mistakes. That's okay because mistakes are part of the learning process as long as you work to see and correct your mistakes. However, when you start *The Program* this may produce some strange results. I went on a second date with a girl, and I made some mistakes from admitting that my last girlfriend broke my heart to telling her I liked The Smiths. The Smiths sing gloomy music and by admitting I liked them, I was projecting to her that I was a gloomy guy. When I reviewed the date I realized it was not a terrible performance, but there was room for improvement. When I called her the next day I got her machine. I left a message asking her to a concert later in the week. By now, you know that this was also a mistake. Instead of asking her for a date on the message, I should have asked her to call me back. The next day I received a message saying she was not interested in me romantically, but she would still go to the concert with me and could I speak to her about a volunteer program which I mentioned I was involved in. Huh?

When you begin *The Program,* girls are going to sometimes end up on the fence about whether they are into you. The way to handle this situation is to pull back a little. If she wants to go on a pretend date as a friend, that is okay. Go on the date but make it casual. Instead of kissing her good-bye, shake her hand. Dress nicely but treat her the way you really would treat a friend. If she calls or emails you, reply to her, but not right away. Wait a couple of days. After your pretend date don't contact her for a week or two. Then call her and ask her out on another date. When you ask her out again specifically ask "Can I take you out on another date?" The worse she can say is no, but she probably will not. When you go out with her again, try not to mess it up this time.

Section Three: How *The Program* Works Day to Day and a Schedule

Chapter Twenty-Five
Priority

Over the next six weeks I want you to make *The Program* a priority. I think you can handle that. The Typical Guy spends a lot of time thinking about women, dreaming about women, looking at pictures of women and watching TV and movies about women. What do you say you take that time and energy and use it to actually work on getting a woman?

One of the things I noticed about Mr. Wonderful was that he spent a fair amount of time chasing girls. The Typical Guy does not but he does spend a lot of time complaining inwardly and to others about having little luck with women. What a shock that is.

In high school I had a friend who seemingly out of the blue got into skateboarding. This was a bit strange because I never remember him being all that athletically inclined. But for about six months the guy ate, breathed and lived skateboarding. The result was he became a really good skateboarder. A bit later I watched him do the same thing when he took up the guitar. Today he is a really successful musician in a prominent rock band. When I started *The Program* I kept my friend's dedication in mind.

For the first six weeks of *The Program*, limit the amount of TV you watch. When I started *The Program* the only time I watched TV was when I was working on *The Program*. It's not really fair to say I watched TV because it was more like background noise while I did some Program activity. The same thing applies to the internet. Stop surfing unless it concerns *The Program*. The same goes for reading. Read this book, read other books on dating, read books and magazines that will help forward your dating life but that is it. Treat sports the same way. I love sports but when I started *The Program* I limited the amount of time I spent watching sports. I actually would listen to the Mets on the radio while I typed out Opening Emails or planned my next date, but again, this was a type of background noise. If you play video games give them a rest for the next six weeks.

What about work? I am not suggesting that you should quit your job and become a bum. However, I am suggesting that for the first six weeks while you get *The Program* up and running, give it priority over work. You should certainly show up to work on time, but how about you also leave work on time? Would you rather make $70,000 a year and be miserable and alone or make $60,000 a year and have a beautiful girlfriend? You know the answer. I am also going to tell you something that you already know, but maybe don't want to admit. When you struggle socially you are not doing your career any favors.

You need to treat your social life the same way. I want you for next six weeks to gear every social event towards successfully meeting women. Single guys in their twenties and their early thirties tend to go out in groups to bars with the idea that they will meet and hook up with girls. How is that working out for you? That good, huh? Why not attend singles events with your friends or a speed dating event or any type of event that offers you better odds at meeting women who will go on dates with you?

This also means that in the next six weeks you skip the events that do not help you with dating. Do not go to the movies, unless it is on a date. Do not attend your uncle's birthday party unless your uncle's party is going to be attended by a lot of single women. The same goes for guy's night out or your weekly poker game. These events will all be around after you have spent the next six weeks mastering *The Program*.

I might even suggest that you cash in a sick day or two and take a long weekend to really start *The Program* at full speed. The most important thing is to start *The Program* as soon as you are done with this book and then to fully and completely commit yourself to it.

Chapter Twenty-Six

Launching The Program

Now the fun begins, the time where, step by step, I show you how to launch and succeed at *The Program*. The best time to start *The Program* is the minute you finish this book. However, for convenience, I assume you are going to start *The Program* on a Friday. Figure on spending most of the first weekend on *The Program*.

On Friday evening dedicate several hours to getting your internet dating profile together. Follow this up Saturday morning by going through your clothes and getting together several outfits for dating. Next, wash and iron these clothes and then place them in their own separate area. These are your dating clothes.

On Saturday afternoon get your hair cut. Check Sunday morning to see if you internet profile has been approved. As soon as it is, write four Opening Emails to four girls that interest you. Each day from here on, you are going to write four Opening Emails. When you receive a response, reply immediately. After you swap emails a couple times, get her number and call to set up a date.

Sunday night is your time to sit down at your computer and do a little research. Find and schedule two singles events for the upcoming week. For the first month or so of *The Program* I want you to do two single events a week.

Once you start going on two dates or more a week you can scale down to one singles event a week.

Each Sunday, write a schedule for *The Program* for the upcoming week. Schedule items such as martial arts classes and times when you will be writing your four Opening Emails each day. Schedule four errands a week that relate to implementing *The Program*. For example, on Monday night after your martial arts class figure on stopping at the drugstore and buying body wash, mints or other items you might need. It would probably be wise to schedule Program Errands on nights when you are not attending a singles event. On nights when you have a singles event, your only Program activity should be completing is your dating site emails.

Program Errands are errands that you complete to help you with *The Program*. Some examples of a Program Errand might be shinning your shoes, shopping for a new shirt for a date outfit, getting a haircut, spending thirty minutes reviewing and improving your internet profile, getting a pair of pants hemmed, washing and ironing your date clothes or getting your teeth cleaned. I recommend reserving the more time consuming Program Errands for the weekend.

During each week within *The Program* you should complete the following items: Your Sunday Program Schedule, attend a martial arts class or two (optional, but recommended), attend two singles events, four Opening Emails each day and four Program Errands. You should also reply to any girls who email you back and when you get a woman sends you her phone number, you should call her the next day and set up a date. After completing the first three weeks of *The Program* you should be going on at least two dates a week. When you achieve this goal, you can scale down from two single events a week to one.

Your Sunday Program Schedule should look something like the following:

Monday
7 P.M. Attend a Martial arts class, 8:30 Program Errand 1) Stop at drugstore on the way home, pick up mouth wash and mints; 9:30 Write four Opening Emails.

Tuesday
6 P.M. Attend martial arts class; 8 Write four Opening Emails.

Wednesday
7 P.M. Attend speed dating event; 9 Write four Opening Emails.

Thursday
7 P.M. Program Errand 2) Buy cologne on internet; 8:30 Write four Opening Emails.

Friday
 9 P.M.: Attend a singles event with a friend; 11 Write four Opening Emails.

Saturday
9 -11:30 A.M. Program Errand 3) Wash and iron date cloths; noon-1 P.M. Program Errand 4) Check out Macy's sale, buy one shirt to upgrade dating cloths; 3:30 Write four Opening Emails.

Sunday 10 A.M. Write four Opening Emails, 7 P.M. Do some research and find two singles events for the upcoming week; 8:45 Write Program Schedule for upcoming week.

When should you deviate from *The Program* Schedule? The answer should be obvious. On date nights, previously scheduled Program activities have to be postponed for another time. The one exception is your Opening Emails. Get those in before or after your date.

Chapter Twenty-Seven

A Day to Day Schedule for The Program

Henry , a twenty-nine year old typical guy, lives on the Upper West Side of Manhattan and just got dumped by his girlfriend. He buys this book, gets inspired and starts *The Program* immediately after finishing this book. In this chapter I will provide a day by day account of how *The Program* proceeded in the first month for Henry. I have included some paragraphs in which I analyze Henry's progress. From reading this account, you can see how *The Program* should proceed on a day by day basis.

First TWO Days

Friday
 5-10 P.M. Henry sets up his profile with pictures.

Saturday
9-11 A.M. Henry goes through his clothes and puts together three date outfits and washes and irons them; Noon-1 P.M. Henry visits a martial arts school, signs up and attends a martial arts class; 1:30-2 P.M. Henry gets a haircut.

Week ONE

Sunday

10 -11 A.M The dating site has approved Henry's profile and pictures and he is up and running. Henry writes four Opening Emails to girls he is interested in.; 6-7:30 P.M. Henry spends an hour on the internet researching and scheduling two single events for the upcoming week. Henry writes his Program Schedule for the upcoming week regarding *The Program.*

Monday
5 P.M. Henry stops at drugstore and picks up body wash, three packs of mints and a comb; 6-7 P.M. Henry attends a martial arts class; 8-9 P.M. Henry writes four Opening Emails to girls he's interested in.

Tuesday
6-7 P.M. Henry attends a trivia night geared toward singles; he gets Tonya's phone number; 7- 8 P.M. Henry writes four Opening Emails; 8-8:15 P.M.: Henry calls Tonya and leaves a message on her machine.

Wednesday
7-8 P.M. Henry writes four Opening Emails.

Thursday
 7:30 P.M. Henry attends a speed dating event; 9:30 P.M. Henry goes home and visits the speed dating site. He enters in which girls he was interested in. He picks six of the eight girls he met. (Remember Henry is trying to go out on as many dates as possible; 10 P.M. Henry writes four Opening Emails to girls he's interested in.

Friday

8:15 P.M. Henry shines his date shoes; 8:30 P.M. Henry gets an email back from Jane. Good job! He writes her back immediately; 8:45 P.M. Henry writes four Opening Emails to girls he is interested in.

Saturday
9-11 A.M Henry goes to the dentist and gets his teeth cleaned; 1-2 P.M. Henry attends a martial arts class; 1-2 P.M. Henry writes four Opening Emails to girls he is interested in; Jane has written back again. Henry writes her a reply and at the end of the email asks for her number; 2:30-3 P.M. Henry washes and irons the two date outfits he wore that week.

Week One Summation
In some ways the first week of *The Program* is the hardest and the most frustrating. You are going to be putting in the most time and generally you will not start dating and succeeding with women until about the end of week two. In other ways the first week of *The Program* is the most exciting because it is the time where you will be improving the most. And that is what Henry is doing. He has in a bit more than a week written a good internet profile, upgraded his clothes, upgraded his looks and he is now approaching a lot of women. He is also, through martial arts, improving physically. It should be noted that Henry in the first week is stopping at the drugstore on Monday, shining his shoes on Friday and by getting his teeth cleaned and washing and ironing his date clothes on Saturday, he has completed four Program Errands in his first full week on *The Program*.

In the first week Henry received only one reply to the Opening Emails that he wrote and one phone number. And in fact Tonya will not call him back. So what? Henry is not discouraged because he knows that what matters is that he's on the right track and well on his way towards success.

Week Two

Sunday
7-8 A.M. Henry writes four Opening Emails to girls he's interested in; It looks like no one chose Henry at Thursday's speed dating event. No big deal; 9-11:30 A.M. Henry does volunteer work at his local church helping under privileged kids by coaching basketball; 6-7 P.M. Henry spends an hour on the internet doing research. He schedules two single events for the upcoming week and writes his Program Schedule for the upcoming week.

Monday
6-7 P.M. Henry attends a martial arts class; 8:00-8:15 P.M. Jane has written Henry back again and given Henry her number; 8:15 P.M. Henry calls Jane and gets her machine; he leaves a message; 8:30-9:30 P.M. Henry writes four Opening Emails; 9:30-9:45 P.M. Henry spends fifteen minutes reviewing his internet profile.

Tuesday
8 P.M. Henry attends a singles night where he tries to get two girls' numbers and strikes out twice. Oh the humanity! 9-10 P.M. Henry writes four Opening Emails; 10:30-11 P.M. Henry gets an email back from Rachel, Good job! He writes her back immediately.

Wednesday
7:30-8:30 P.M. Henry writes four Opening Emails; 8:35 P.M. Rachel writes Henry. He immediately writes her back.

Thursday
 7:30 P.M. Henry attends a speed dating event; 9:35 P.M. Henry checks his messages and gets a message from Jane; Henry calls Jane and speaks to her for twenty minutes; she is away for the weekend, but she agrees to meet him for a drink on Monday night; 9:30 P.M. Henry goes home and visits the speed dating sight and enters in which girls he was interested in. He picks six of the eight girls he met; 10 P.M. Henry writes four Opening Emails to girls he is interested in; 10:30 P.M. Kate, who Henry met at speed dating, chooses him. He emails her a note and asks for her number.

Friday
6-7 P.M. Henry attends a martial arts class; 7:15 P.M. Henry picks a copy of *Fit for Life* at a local book store; 7:30-8:30 P.M. Henry writes four original Opening Emails to girls he is interested in; 8:35 P.M.: Rachel writes Henry back. Henry again writes her an email and asks for her number.

Saturday
7- 8:30 A.M. Henry washes and irons two date outfits and then goes to Macy's and buys a pair of slacks and a shirt on sale, thus upgrading one date outfit; 9 A.M.-2 P.M. Henry drives out to Bear Mountain with some friends and goes on a hike; 7-8 P.M.: Henry writes four Opening Emails to girls he's interested in; Kate has written back to Henry with her

phone number. Henry calls her and leaves a message on her machine.

Week Two Summation

Henry is definitely moving in the right direction. In Week two he has yet to go on a date but he has a date lined up with Jane on Monday. In addition it looks like Rachel will give Henry her number and Henry has already gotten Kate's number. As you can see Henry in Week two continues to work hard in every direction. He is getting himself in better shape with karate, attending singles events, emailing a lot of girls and working to improve his image.

He also has completed four more Program Errands. In addition, Henry does some volunteer work. He does this to be a good person and because he enjoys it, but he also volunteers with an eye toward making himself more interesting and thus improving his Dating Personality. On Saturday he goes on a hike with some friends and again Henry partially does this to become a more attractive guy.

Week Three

Sunday

5:00-6 P.M. Henry writes four Opening Emails to girls he's interested in; 6:00-7 P.M. Henry spends an hour on the internet and schedules two single events for the upcoming week; Henry writes his Program Schedule for the upcoming week; 7:00-8 P.M. Kate calls Henry. Henry chats with her for twenty minutes and asks her out; Henry has a date with Kate for Thursday. Good Job, Henry!

Monday

8:00-9 P.M. Henry meets Jane for a drink; 9:30-10:30 P.M. Henry writes four Opening Emails to girls he's interested in; 10:30-10:45 P.M. Henry reads the first chapter of *Fit for Life*.

Tuesday
6:00-7 P.M. Henry attends a martial arts class; 7:00-7:30 P.M. Rachel has written Henry back with her number. He calls her and leaves a message; 7:00-8 P.M. Henry writes four Opening Emails; 8:30 P.M. Henry calls Jane to arrange to go out to dinner on Friday night. Henry has a second date. Good job!

Wednesday
7:30 P.M. Henry attends an arts event for singles; he approaches two women and they both shoot him down. Oh the humanity! 8:45 P.M. Henry stops at the drugstore and buys some mouth wash and mints; 9:00-10 P.M.: Henry writes four Opening Emails to girls he's interested in; 10:00-10:15 P.M. Belinda writes back; Henry immediately replies.

Thursday
8:30-9:30 P.M. Henry goes out on a date with Kate; 10-11 P.M. Henry writes four Opening Emails to girls he's interested in; 11 P.M. Henry received an email back from Christi. He writes her back immediately.

Friday
5-6 P.M. Henry writes four Opening Emails to girls he's interested in; 8-10 P.M. Henry goes to dinner with Jane and the two have a great time. Henry ends by making out with her a bit before she goes up to her apartment.

Saturday

9-10:30 A.M. Henry washes and irons his date clothes; Noon-1 P.M. Henry attends a martial arts class; 2 P.M. Henry is not that crazy about Kate, but he remembers it's important to date a lot; he calls her and asks her out again. She agrees to meet him at an outdoor concert in the park on Monday night; 2:40 P.M. Henry received a message from Rachel while he was out the night before. He calls her and leaves a message; 2:45 P.M.: Belinda emails Henry and he emails her back; he asks for her number; 2:45-3 P.M. Henry shines his shoes; 6-10 P.M. Henry attends a booze cruise with a friend geared towards singles. He meets a girl named Janet and gets her number; 11:30-12 P.M. A slightly buzzed Henry writes four Opening Emails to girls he's interested in.

Week Three Summation

As you can see things are beginning to roll for Henry in Week three. He went on a total of three dates with two different girls. He also is trading phone calls with Rachel and emailing back and forth with Belinda and Christi. And he has a date set up with Kate. There are a couple of things we can learn from Henry here. Henry decides to give Kate a second chance even though he is at least not initially all that into her. This is very important. First, Henry has to improve his dating skills and the only way to do this is to date a lot. Second, first impressions are often wrong.

During Henry's second date with Jane she tells him briefly about an on again off again relationship which she has just ended. Henry listens to her, does not change the subject or act uncomfortable and expresses some sympathy.

Later he mentions that he just broke up with his girlfriend. While literally true, it is spin because she in fact dumped him, but Henry knows the importance of conveying to his date that he has The Quality. It is important to note that Henry is not shutting down *The Program* even though he really likes Jane and Jane appears to be really into him. In fact Henry goes out on a booze cruise type singles events the night after he goes on a second date with Jane.

We can also take note that one of Henry's Program Errands is reading a chapter of the book *Fit for Life*. A Program Errand can be something as simple as doing a bit of reading.

Week Four

Sunday
7:00-7:30 A.M. Henry writes four Opening Emails to girls he's interested in; 9:00-11:30 A.M. Henry does volunteer work at his local church helping under privileged kids by coaching basketball; 6:30 P.M. Henry gets an email back from Belinda with her number; he calls her and sets up a date on Thursday night; 7 P.M. Henry calls Janet and they agree to meet for a drink at a happy hour spot not far from where they both work on Wednesday; 8-9 P.M. Henry spends an hour on the internet doing research. He schedules one singles event for the upcoming week and writes a schedule for the upcoming week regarding *The Program*.

Monday
7:30-9 P.M. Henry meets Kate for dinner; 9:10 P.M. Henry gets a call from Jane; she says she had a great time with him but her on again off boyfriend has called her, and she

wants to give him another chance; this news hurts a bit but Henry resists the urge to feel sorry for himself; in fact, he goes home and writes four Opening Emails to girls he's interested in and then spends a half hour upgrading his internet profile.

Tuesday

8- 9:30 P.M. Henry attends a party at a bar for the birthday of a former college buddy. There he sees Lisa, who never seemed all that into him. Henry chats with her and then mentions that a work buddy of his is single and that he thinks the two of them would really hit it off. Lisa gives Henry her number and later Henry emails the number to his buddy; 10 P.M. Gaby has winked at Henry. He immediately reads her profile and sends her an email; 10-10:30 P.M. Henry writes four Opening Emails; 10:30 P.M. Christi emails Henry back and Henry replies asking for her number.

Wednesday

6:30 P.M. Henry meets Janet for a couple drinks at a happy hour spot; 7:30 to 8:30 P.M. Henry writes four Opening Emails to girls he's interested in; 8:30-9 P.M. Henry gets email responses from three different girls, Heather, Beth, and Gina; Henry emails back each of them. He feels he is getting much better at writing Opening Emails.

Thursday

7:30 P.M. Henry takes Belinda for espresso and dessert in little Italy; 10 P.M. Henry writes four Opening Emails to girls he's interested in; 10:30 P.M. Gaby writes Henry back and Henry emails her and asks for her number.

Friday
6-7 P.M. Henry attends a martial arts class; 8:30-9:30 P.M. Henry writes four Opening Emails to girls he's interested in.

Saturday
9-10:30 A.M. Henry washes and irons his three date outfits; 1 P.M. Henry gets a haircut; 6-10 P.M. With a friend, Henry attends a booze cruise geared towards singles. He meets a girl named Erica and gets her number; 11:30-12 P.M. A slightly buzzed Henry writes four Opening Emails four to girls he's interested in.

Week Four Summation
Henry tries a number of singles events with little success. However, at the end of the third week, he attends a booze cruise event and has some success. The following week he attends the same event and again has success. The point is that it might take a bit of experimenting to find a singles event that yields dates, but once you find an event that works, milk it for all its worth. Henry gets dumped by Jane and this hurts a little. However, Henry resists the urge to mope and continues to work hard at *The Program*. When you get dumped in *The Program* it is important that you do the same.

In week four Henry attends a party for an old college buddy. Henry makes a point of attending this party because he knows parties are a good place to meet women. There Henry sets up one of his work friends on a date. Later Henry will mention to his work friend that he hopes he will return the favor.

Around week three is the period where you should actually start going on two to three dates a week. If it gets too hectic you can scale down to one singles event a week. As you can see Henry in week four only attends one singles event. It's important to remember that while you are dating you must continue to pursue other girls.

One of the things that the above schedule reveals is how much *The Program* is a numbers game. In *The Program* you are approaching a lot of women and you end up dating only a small percentage of the girls you actually approach. In the first two weeks Jane, Nicole and Betty all responded to Henry's Opening dating emails, however, even though he always responded promptly he only ended going on a date with Jane. In the first week Henry also attended one speed dating event and one singles event which yielded one phone number and ultimately no dates. In the second week he got responses from Gaby, Heather, and Sue but Henry still does not date anyone. However, by week three Henry is really rolling.

Some Other Things to Note

Percentage wise, Henry does not get many responses to his Opening Emails. However, because he is writing four Opening Emails a day he ends up getting a lot of dates. As he gains more experience his percentage rate goes up.

Henry's experience also illustrates that a major source of dates are second and third dates (women Henry asks out again.) In some cases Henry does this reluctantly but he understands that it's important.

I did not mention The Review Process in Henry's schedule. However, at the end of each date, Henry mentally reviews what he did wrong and what worked. He also periodically reviews in his mind each aspect of his performance in *The Program.*

The Review Process is an indispensable part of *The Program.*

Chapter Twenty-Eight

Day to Day aspects of The Program: Ups and Downs and the Nature of Change

In *The Program*, as with most things, if you are not moving forward you are likely moving backward. With this in mind, you want to constantly have an eye out toward improvement and innovation. You should read whatever you can that might give you an edge at dating, talk about dating with your friends and constantly keep an eye out for ways to improve.

There is always more to learn and there is absolutely no shame in trying to learn more. At one point I was attending a speed dating event and I could tell I was not doing well. The guy next to me who I had seen at previous events seemed to be doing quite well. At the end of the event, I bought him a beer and picked his brain a bit concerning speed dating. In return, I gave him some advice on internet dating, which was working well for me.

When Mr. Wonderful was shopping for a new car he asked twenty different women what car they thought was the hottest. What this teaches is that Mr. Wonderful was always searching for an even greater edge.

During the first six weeks of *The Program,* work at it furiously. Studying Henry's schedule shows you how to do that. After the initial sprint, you have to find the right balance that allows you to keep going over the long haul with *The Program*. Part of this occurs naturally because the more you practice at implementing *The Program*, the more skilled and efficient you become at implementing it. I found a cheap place to get my clothes dry cleaned in my neighborhood and every other week I would drop off my date clothes there. At one point I cut back on the number of dates I scheduled. Considering my previous sorry dating history, this almost borders on parody. It was a bit like a guy who has been starving for years moving to a new country where food was so plentiful that he started to worry about becoming obese. After a month or two into *The Program*, you may conclude that you will be better off going on two dates a week instead of three. You may also want to scale down from two singles events a week to one. Because of increasing skill and efficiency after the initial six weeks in *The Program*, you should be able to scale down from four Program Errands a week to two or three.

One of the ways to improve and become more efficient at *The Program* is to be as organized as possible. We already touched on this a little in the discussion about improving your appearance, but it applies to all other areas of *The Program* as well. I suggest keeping a notebook on your desk next to your computer. Use this notebook to write down the names and numbers of the women you are dating. You should also note the place and times of your dates. Another good thing to note would be cool places such as bars and restaurants that you discover that would be good for dates. Follow a strict rule that this notebook never leaves your desk. Losing it would obviously be terrible. When you get a girl's number, immediately store the number in both your phone and your notebook.

The Program will get easier as time goes by as long as you are working hard at it. With time your skills at internet dating will improve. You will also find that it's taking you less time to write Opening Emails, and your response rate will definitely improve. Also due to the martial arts and your work with regards to dressing and eating healthier, your appearance will improve, which of course always makes things easier. Finally, and most importantly, your Dating Personality will improve and this will help immeasurably. In short, working at *The Program* will improve your entire dating life.

You can expect to go through an occasional dry spell in *The Program*. I am a New York Mets fan. David Wright is one of their best players. In his first five seasons he had a batting average of 309 with 27 home runs per full season. Even he has weeks where he strikes out a lot and gets only a few hits and no home runs. He keeps on working. The same goes for *The Program*. You are going to get the occasional week where you go on a date with a girl and she is not that into you, the girl who went on a second date does not want to go on a third date and you are having little luck with internet dating. Just keep soldiering on. Remember with *The Program* there are going to be a lot more good weeks than bad.

When you do have a bad week in *The Program,* I also suggest that you engage in a thorough review as to how you might improve things.

I am now going to run the risk of getting a little philosophical. Successfully completing *The Program* will represent a fairly significant change in your life. Change is hard. When you make a major change, life has a way of getting in the way. You may have seen this if you have ever been on a diet or tried to quit smoking.

As an example, take the decision to quit smoking. You decide to quit smoking and you manage to go two weeks without smoking a cigarette. Then your boss starts putting a lot of pressure on you at work. You get stressed out and start smoking again. When I first started *The Program* after about a month, I saw that it was working well for me, and I was pretty excited about the direction I was going. Over the last ten days, I had gone out on three dates, and I was trading calls with two other girls. This was during flu season in New York, and I got really sick. I was forced to stop *The Program* for a full week. When I finally recovered, I had to start over again. I didn't like it, but I did it. If life knocks you down, pick yourself up, brush the dust off and keep going.

Concluding Chapters

Chapter Twenty-Nine
Questions You might Have and Some Specific Advice for College Students

The Program sounds like it is time consuming. Do you have any tips if time is an issue?
The short answer is yes, *The Program* is somewhat time consuming. However, how badly do you want to succeed at dating? Do really have anything better to do with your time? It's also true that *The Program* becomes easier and a little less time consuming as you work at it.

The longer answer is that if time is a real issue, there is some flexibility time-wise built into *The Program*. In the example schedule I provide, Henry goes to martial arts classes three times a week. However, you can get away with attending martial arts classes once or twice a week or not at all. In *The Program* I am suggesting you attend two singles events a week. If time is a real issue you might be able to get away with attending one singles event a week. Remember you are only supposed to be spending about fifty minutes at each singles event anyway. As I mentioned in a previous chapter, I also found being organized and planning ahead saves time.

Will The Program cost me a lot of money?

No. In fact I have tried to emphasize that throwing around money in an effort to improve your dating life is self defeating. Spending a lot of money on dates, flowers, and gifts will actually hinder your efforts in *The Program*. Most single events are either free or fairly moderately priced. I would not attend those that are too pricey. In this book I urge you to minimize your drinking which is also very cost effective. Finally, improving the way you dress does not have to be very costly, if you shop around a bit you should be able to find great looking clothes at reasonable prices. Some of this depends on your previous dating strategy. If it consisted of you going out to bars and trying to meet women there, then you will save money; however, if your current strategy consists of staying at home, watching TV, and complaining a lot, then *The Program* will probably cost you a little more money.

Do you have any tips about starting The Program in the best way possible?

I would definitely dedicate the first two weekends to *The Program*, and I suggest you cash in a sick day or two and make one or both of these weekends a long weekend.

Can I change a few things in *The Program* and expect to succeed?

Sorry, but you really cannot. Look, when it comes to dating and attracting women, if you only needed to make a couple changes, you would have figured out what these changes were and made them some time ago. When you decide to take up *The Program*, you have to follow it as closely as you possibly can.

Can I call up girls who I dated in the past?

Yes, but you have to keep it in perspective. Following up with a girl who has broken up with you in the past is not a terrible idea. In a way she is just another potential date. And that is just the way you have to think about her. Wait about two months after the break up before calling her. Chat with her and then early in the conversation ask if she has a boyfriend. Do this even if you have heard through the grapevine or on Facebook that she does not have a boyfriend. If the answer is yes, there is really no point in going much further. If the answer is no, follow up with mock surprise "Now how can that possibly be. The guys in this town must all be blind!" Then change the subject and shortly thereafter ask her out on a date. When you ask her out don't say something like "Do you want to give me another chance?" or "Do you want to see if second time's the charm?" Just ask her out. You don't want to say anything that reminds her she dumped you and indicates to her that you do not have The Quality. If she says yes that is great. You got another date. If she says no, well it was a long shot anyway and her loss.

I am not a CEO, a rock star, or an heir to a large fortune. Will this hurt me with regards to Leadership?

No. It will not hurt you. Most single guys are not CEOs, rock stars, or heirs to large fortunes. Most single guys are architects, real estate agents, contractors, students, teachers, small businessmen, salesmen, etc. Most CEO's by the time they get to be a CEO are long married and when they were single they were just guys with a dream. Showing leadership is nothing more than acting like a man and not displaying Fear Based Behavior. When it comes to your job, it's important that you present it in a positive light and that you present yourself as a man with a future.

Should I do The Program with my single friend or roommate?

Absolutely. first a little friendly competition never hurt anybody, and second, having someone to attend singles events with is a good idea.

If I go out on a date with a woman and I sense that she is just not that into me should I ask her out again?

If that happens, the odds are that your instincts are correct. That said, you should absolutely call her the next day and ask her out again. *The Program* is partially a numbers game and sometimes you will ask a girl out again who broadcasts all the wrong vibes but turns out to be really into you.

There is also a trick you can try on occasion. Call her and say you really like her, but you feel it would better if the two of you could just be friends. Then hang out with her as a friend and see if she starts chasing you. If she does not start chasing you, dump her as a friend as well.

Should I read other dating books?

Definitely, you want to be constantly looking for any information to improve your skills. The two dating books that I found to be most helpful were actually the two that differed most from a philosophy standpoint. I thought *"The Game"* by Neil Strauss had some very helpful ideas. I also really liked a lesser known book called *"How To Make Every Girl Want You"* by John Fate. I did not buy into either philosophy completely but I found aspects of both books very helpful. *The Program* is somewhat like the Buddhism of Dating Books in that it works very well with other dating books.

You should also read magazine articles on dating and even attend the occasional seminar or lecture on the subject.

How should I handle dating advice from friends and family?

The best thing to do with dating advice from friends and family is to try it out. The great thing about *The Program* is you have plenty of opportunities to try out their advice.

If I am struggling with my weight do you have any points to emphasize and any additional advice?

There are two different problems which may arise for guys on *The Program* who struggle with their weight. The first is that it may take a bit longer for you to start going on a lot of dates. If this happens just be patient and keep working. Eventually you will start succeeding. With the weight loss program and the martial arts, you will be getting into much better shape fairly quickly.

The second problem you may have is just the opposite. After a few weeks you may end up going on so many dates that you get a little cocky and you start to skip out on your martial arts and Weight Watchers meetings. Do not do this because it will catch up with you. In *The Program* you have to keep moving forward both physically and mentally. I realize that adding a weekly Weight Watchers meeting will add to your schedule. If you really need to, you can count this as one of your two single events.

I am finding that with The Program I can easily go on two to three dates a week just through internet dating. Should I bother attending single events?

This happened to me and I discovered that you definitely should also attend singles events. One of the things you have to practice and get good at in *The Program* is approaching women and you do not really get the opportunity to do this with internet dating. Definitely attend at least one singles event a week.

If I am in college and would like to do The Program would you have any additional advice?

The dynamics of *The Program* would basically remain the same. Singles events would be replaced by college type social events and going out with friends. I would still employ the use of internet dating although I would try to find a site that skews a bit younger. Do some research and see which dating site in your area attracts the most women around your age.

Make a point of studying the social events you are attending and steering yourself to the events with the best prospects for meeting women. It would probably be helpful to find a friend or a roommate to join you in *The Program*. College students might find having a good wingman to be particularly helpful. Look to join college activities with an eye towards meeting women such as student politics, volunteer work, co-ed intramural sports, etc. When you write your Program Schedule on Sunday night be sure to pencil in both your planned college social events and college activities that you are doing with an eye towards meeting women.

If I am in high school can *The Program* still help me?

Yes, but obviously with some adjustments which leads us to our next chapter.

Chapter Thirty

If You Are younger, Read this Chapter

If you are in high school there are some adjustments which have to be made in *The Program* and some points to emphasize. In the place of singles events, attend school dances and other social gatherings geared toward kids your age. Some of these events may have a reputation for being uncool—attend them anyway. When it comes to attending these events use the instructions I have outlined in Chapter Eighteen on singles events as a guideline

Join activities with an eye toward meeting girls. When you choose an activity, the most important factor to take into account is the potential to meet girls. If it turns out to have too many guys, switch to another activity. Some activities that might work are prom committee, student newspaper, yearbook committee or student government. When it comes to geek activities such as science club or math club, unless by some miracle one of these activities is full of hot girls, avoid them like the plague. If you are already in one of these club, quit it *posthaste*. Computer clubs are a grey area and you have to take into account that this activity might one day get you really rich.

Figure out which activities draw girls and attend those events. When it comes to choosing activities be smart about it. Obviously joining the football team does not directly lead to meeting women, but it might increase your social status, get you in shape and serve as a pipeline to getting you invited to some cool parties.

When you consider activities, keep in mind two requirements: the potential to meet girls and the potential that you can succeed at the activity. Women are attracted to success and leadership. If you have no inclination towards acting you might want to skip drama club despite all the hot actress chicks. You might find that something like the student newspaper is more up your alley.

Overall, work on being well liked and popular. I would pick up and read a book by Dale Carnegie called "*How to Make Friends and Influence People*." Churches tend to sponsor youth groups and you should check them out. In the summer consider becoming a camp councilor at a coed camp. This will offer you a great opportunity to meet other female camp councilors who are your age.

If you are musically inclined, get involved in or start a rock band. When it comes to choosing music to play your band should play fun music that girls will actually like. For every original song you perform, play two cover tunes. If you play an instrument such as the violin I want you to put down this book, go get your violin, open a rear window in your house, look both ways to make sure no one is back there and then toss the violin out the window. I have some news for you, no one has ever gotten laid playing the violin. Next find a guitar, learn to play that and go find or start a rock band. Trust me after learning to play the violin, learning to play the guitar will be cake. Keith Richards, the guitarist for The Rolling Stones, is in his 60s and he is still getting laid.

Here are some additional points which should be emphasized:

Regarding the way you dress— make a conscious decision to dress better and work hard at it.

You are at an age where your skin can be terrible. If you have this problem, go to the doctor and get the medication that is needed to get it under control.

Definitely take up martial arts. In fact I would argue that it is even more important at your age. Particularly if you are being picked on. If that is the case, attend a martial arts class at least five or six times a week, and then in a couple of months start to stand up for yourself. If you have to, kick someone's ass. No one has the right to bully you. If you are being bullied *choose* a martial art that is more aggressive such as karate.

If you are struggling with your weight, get into a weight loss program and work hard at it every day. Also, make it a point to take martial arts classes four to five times a week.

Chat up girls and then ask them out on dates. I know you are at an age where most kids hang out in groups and maybe hook up at parties. Great—do that too, but by going on dates you are putting yourself at an advantage. When it comes to going on dates obviously you are not going to spend a lot which is fine. This gives you an opportunity to be more creative. Chapter Twenty-Two suggests some ideas that are pretty affordable. Being in high school gives you additional options such as football games and dances.

Remember the concept discussed in Working the Room. It is important to put this concept into practice at parties, dances, and other social events.

Take a look at the way you use humor. There is a major difference between being funny and charming and being the class clown. Pay attention to the way The Mr. Wonderfuls in your social circle use humor. Take note of the fact that they use humor in way that makes them look good. There may be a tendency at your age to act in a way that draws attention to yourself whether that attention is good or bad. This is something you should examine and change.

For a teen on the first week of *The Program,* your Sunday Program Schedule should look something like this:

Monday
After school, quit the science club. Instead join the year book club which has some cute girls in it.

Tuesday
 After school, sign up for and attend a martial arts class. Go to the doctor get some pills and medicated pads for your skin.

Wednesday
After school, put up your violin for sale on eBay. Get a guitar and meet with a couple of equally musically inclined friends and start your rock band.

Thursday
After school, attend a martial arts class, go home and start sorting and washing your clothes. Tell your mother you want to go shopping for some new cloths, but before you go, do some research on the topic. If you can, bring an older sister or some else who has a good fashion sense.

Friday

Attend a school dance, talk to boys and girls (Work the Room). Be social, try asking one girl out to the movies on Saturday.

Saturday
9 A.M. Get clothes ready for date, attend a martial arts class, get a cool haircut, get ready and be on time for your date.

Sunday
Check out the church youth group that your mother has been bugging you about. Maybe it's a good place to meet girls. Spend twenty minutes online researching potential camps to work at in the summer. In the afternoon, practice with your band. At 8:45 P.M. write a Program Schedule for the upcoming week.

Chapter Thirty-One

Next

If you are younger and you are planning to go away to college, you should follow the advice in this chapter. Its purpose is to help you stack the odds in your favor during your college years. In dating you do not get points for degree of difficulty. There are a number of colleges which were traditionally for women but now admit men. These colleges tend to be mostly attended by women to the tune of better than eighty percent. Make a point of finding and attending one of these schools. You want to pick a college where the women are literally throwing themselves at you.

When you get out of college you are going to have two major concerns, your job and women. Trust me when I tell you that you are going to spend a lot more time thinking about women. If you graduate from college having learned to successfully date women you will have gotten far more from college than anyone else I know.

This advice applies doubly for computer/engineering/math/science guys. There is a good chance you are thinking about attending an elite computer/engineering/math/science school that has about eight guys for every girl. ARE YOU NUTS? HAVE YOU LOST YOUR MIND? Do you want to be as miserable with women for the next four years as you are now? The type of schools that I am recommending have also have computer/

engineering/math/science programs. If the school has a lesser reputation in whatever field you specialize in, so what? Most of the guys in these technical fields are going to have a much easier road to plough career wise than socially.

One thing you can count on. Your parents are going to push you to attend the wrong kind of college. Dig in your heels on this one. Do not even apply to a school unless it has the correct ratio of guys to girls. Be up front with your parents and remember that they were single once too. You're a normal straight young man who's interested in women. That's absolutely nothing to be ashamed of. My advice is not about getting laid. It is about learning to have healthy relationships with women.

Explain to your parents what a tough time you've had with dating girls. It should not be a shock to you when I tell you they've noticed that you took your cousin to Junior Prom. You might appeal to your Dad and remind him how tough it was to date and to be single before he got married. This would never have worked for me. I get the impression that my father was very good at dating when he was single. In my case, the apple did not just fall from the tree, it landed in a different zip code. Both your parents want grandchildren, particularly your mother. Explain to them that the odds of them getting grandchildren are a lot better if you figure out this whole women thing in college. If you are a computer/engineering/math/science guy you might also mention that the field you are attending after college is fairly male dominated and meeting women after college is going to present even more of a challenge than it does now.

When I was seventeen I applied to five colleges in the northeast. One of the schools that accepted me was a relatively unknown college in Connecticut. It was a former all girls school that had just started to accept men. There were about nine girls for every guy there. The school was my safety school and they actually offered me the best financial aid package. I chose to attend a school with a better reputation. To this day, this is one of the biggest regrets of my life. If I'd had any idea of the amount frustration that was to follow for the next fifteen years, I would have crawled from New York to Connecticut to attend that college.

An architect I worked with attended an elite New York college a year after they started to accept men. He said that college had about five men for every ninety-five girls and about half the guys there were gay. As you might imagine, he found college to be a really fun time. If only I'd known. I ended up graduating from a college in New York with a good reputation, good enough that when people find out what school I attended, they are impressed. You know what? That and $2.75 will get me on the subway.

Don't make the mistake I made. Attend a school with the correct ratio of women to men. When you get out of college, would you rather earn fifty thousand a year and have a beautiful girlfriend or earn sixty thousand a year and sit at home at night all alone because you fail miserably with women? Think hard about how you would answer that question.

My advice: attend the correct type of college, get good grades and study hard. Also read *The Program* and work hard at it as well.

Chapter Thirty-Two

Closing The Program

When you should close *The Program* down? The answer is simple—when you have an exclusive girlfriend.

This does not mean you should close *The Program* when you have met a girl you want to be your exclusive girlfriend. Closing *The Program* before she is truly your exclusive girlfriend will hurt your chances of her actually becoming your exclusive girlfriend for reasons which were explained in earlier portions of the book.

When you know for certain she is your exclusive girlfriend, it's time to shut *The Program* down. Good job, by the way! Start by shutting down your internet dating profile. Before you do that, just on the off chance that she is not the one-and-only, cut and paste your written profile and save it on your computer. Also do the same with your profile pictures. Dating new people and attending singles events obviously come to a halt, but do not throw out the baby with the bath water. Remember why you were able to attract her in the first place, the practices of building up your confidence, keeping your body in shape, presenting yourself in the best light and dressing well. Continue all those things.

And finally having achieved success with *The Program* be happy, appreciative and treat your new girlfriend with kindness and appreciation. If the unthinkable happens and your relationship comes to an end, don't waste time moping. Restart *The Program* immediately. DO NOT put off restarting *The Program* because you have hopes of reuniting with your ex girlfriend. Getting back in *The Program* will actually improve the chances of getting her back.

Chapter Thirty-Three

Conclusion

There are some customs in dating, but no set rules. This actually makes it very different from most things. College, high school, work, and computer programming are all governed by established rules. Even marriage has rules that are accepted by most couples: No cheating, the kids take the husband's last name, the man drives on family trips and so on. The lack of rules at times drives men out of their minds. Men like watching baseball precisely because it is an extremely orderly activity based on a strict rule book and a group of umpires whose decisions are ironclad. Women like soap operas. Sit down and watch one sometime and see if you can figure out any set rules.

The lack of rules in dating make it much more of an art than science. A portion of *The Program* involves learning a set of skills such as dressing well, speaking well of yourself and so on. However, a large portion of this book is directed at getting you into a position to gain a lot of experience with women and for you to learn from this experience.

Dating is a relatively new phenomenon. Up until about a one hundred years ago a large portion of all marriages were arranged. Even when men and women courted each other it was limited. Life expectancies were much shorter and if men and women had waited until their late twenties and beyond to get married and have children it's questionable whether the species would have survived. Even today marriages are arranged for large numbers of people in India and Muslim countries. India alone has about a sixth of the world's population.

Dating is still alive, well and expanding here in the West. Fewer and fewer people meet someone early and marry them. The end of the sexual revolution means not as many people are jumping in bed together and more and more are actually getting to know each other. You need to figure out how to become good at dating and to enjoy it because the odds are you'll be doing it for a while.

Do not use *The Program* as an avenue to become a bad guy. Treat the women in your life with decency and respect. Do not become that guy who is really good with women and takes advantage and behaves terribly. You have to date a lot of women in order get a girlfriend and hopefully eventually a wife but that does not mean you should turn into a sleazy guy.

To close, let me remind you once again that I did not create the rules of *The Program*. I simply observed what was happening and described what I saw. With this in mind, I leave you with the final lesson from Mr. Wonderful. When he was single, he was always a stand up guy. Now that he's married to an amazing women and is a devoted husband, he is still a stand up guy.

Start *The Program*, work hard at it and get out there and have fun.

Glossary

The 24-Hour Rule When you meet a girl and get her number, you have twenty four hours to call her and ask her out

.

The 50-Minute Rule When you go to a singles events or a bar figure on being there fifty minutes to an hour at the most.

The 55-Hour Rule After you go out with a women a couple times The 24-Hour Rule changes to The 55-Hour Rule. After a second date with a girl you have 55 hours to call her and ask her out again.

Dating Act A group of stories and jokes that you refine and use with women you are dating or interested in dating. When you are on a date, pay attention to which stories and jokes get a good reaction. These stories and jokes should become part of your Dating Act.

Dating Personality Your Dating Personality is how you act, speak, communicate and carry yourself in front of women who you are dating or are interested in dating.

Fear Based Behavior The behavior that The Typical Guy displays in front of women. He is both interested in and afraid of her. Fear Based Behavior occurs when a guy is interested in a woman and his actions indicated to her that he is afraid of her. Some examples of Fear Based Behavior are when you are with a woman and you put yourself down, act nervous in front of her or tell her how lucky you are to be with her. Fear Based Behavior must be avoided.

The First Chance You Get Rule If on an internet dating site you receive an email from a girl, you have two hours to respond to that email. In most cases you should answer the email   as soon as you read it.

Leadership Women are attracted to men who display Leadership. In *The Program* it is important that you display leadership when you are with women you are dating or are attracted to.

Mr. Wonderful A single guy who excels at dating and attracting women to such a degree that it appears the entire process comes naturally to him.

Opening Email The initial email which you send to women on dating internet sites whose profile has caught your eye.

Program Errand An errand that you do to help you with *The Program*. Some examples of might be shinning your shoes, shopping for a new shirt for a date outfit, getting a haircut, or spending thirty minutes reviewing and improving your internet profile.

Program Schedule In *The Program* each Sunday night you should write a Program Schedule in which you map out your program activities for the upcoming week.

The Quality The characteristic that women initially find most attractive in a man is their ability to attract a lot of women. In *The Program* I refer to this as The Quality. An important part of *The Program* is that women you are interested in perceive that you have The Quality.

The Review Process Every interaction you have with a woman should be examined and reviewed so you can see what you were doing right and what you need to improve. You will make mistakes in implementing *The Program*. That's okay. What's important is that you recognize those mistakes and change them. The Review Process does not just apply to dates but to every aspect and stage of dating.

The Typical Guy A single guy who struggles with dating and attracting women to various degrees.

Working the Room When you attend a singles event or other social event, introduce yourself and chat with both men and women. Force yourself to be very social.

About the Author

Joseph Adago

The Program
Master the Art of Dating and Attracting Women in Six Weeks

Joseph Adago has worked in New York City Real Estate marketing and sales for the last ten years. During this time he has sold millions of dollars worth of real estate and rented scores of high end apartments. He currently works as a top real estate agent in arguably the hottest neighborhood in the country, Williamsburg, Brooklyn.

After struggling with being single for years, Joseph Adago used his expertise at real estate sales and marketing to devise a system that shows men how to wildly succeed at another kind of marketing: dating and attracting women. The result is The Program: Master the Art of Dating and Attracting Women in Six Weeks, a book that will revolutionize dating for men.

Last year, Joseph Adago used his own system to break out of his dating rut. During this time he met and dated a number of amazing women. Through his system, he also met the wonderful woman he recently married. He lives in Park Slope, Brooklyn with his wife Olivia.

To contact Joe or to read more about him and his work, visit his website at:
http://www.joesdatingprogram.com/

To visit Joe's award winning dating blog:
http://joesdatingprogram.wordpress.com/